ENTERPRISE DASHBOARDS

ENTERPRISE DASHBOARDS

DESIGN AND BEST PRACTICES FOR IT

SHADAN MALIK

WILEY

John Wiley & Sons, Inc.

Copyright © 2005 by John Wiley & Sons, Inc. All rights reserved.

Published by John Wiley & Sons, Inc., Hoboken, New Jersey.
Published simultaneously in Canada.

For general information on our other products and services, or technical support, please contact our Customer Care Department within the United States at 800-762-2974, outside the United States at 317-572-3993 or fax 317-572-4002.

Wiley also publishes its books in a variety of electronic formats. Some content that appears in print may not be available in electronic books.

For more information about Wiley products, visit our Web site at *www.wiley.com.*

All the illustrations and dashboard examples throughout the book are based on fictitious data, and do not reflect any organization's real performance, past or present.

Library of Congress Cataloging-in-Publication Data

Malik, Shadan.
  Enterprise dashboards : design and best practices for IT / Shadan Malik.
     p.   cm.
  Includes index.
   ISBN-13 978-0-471-73806-0 (cloth)
   ISBN-10 0-471-73806-9 (cloth)
  1. Dashboards (Management information systems)   I. Title.
HD30.213.M34 2005
658.4′038′011—dc22
                                                    2005007458

Printed in the United States of America
10 9 8 7 6 5 4 3 2 1

To Aleena, Shifa, and My Mother

CONTENTS

Preface   ix

Acknowledgments   xv

About the Contributors   xvii

PART ONE   Dashboard Execution   **1**

1   Business Case for Enterprise Dashboards   3
2   Dashboarding Process: The Meta-Information 15
3   The Audience   35
4   Presentation: Design, Layout, and Navigation 45
5   Dashboard Alerts   59
6   Storyboarding   69
7   Project Planning and Branding   87

PART TWO   Dashboard Types   **95**

8   Dashboard Categories   97
9   Divisional Dashboards   113

PART THREE Dashboard Software Assessment **145**

10 Software Features   147
11 Software Acquisition and ROI   165

PART FOUR Case Studies   **175**

12 DaimlerChrysler Sales and Marketing Dashboard   177
13 ING DIRECT Executive Dashboard   187
14 Dashboard in Health Care (Emergency Medical Associates) 197

Index   **209**

PREFACE

The term *dashboard* brings to mind that panel under the windshield of a vehicle that contains indicator dials, various compartments, and control instruments. Its beauty lies in its functionality. It brings together all of the relevant data and functions within easy accessibility to the driver. It allows us to monitor important, even lifesaving data while performing the vital day-to-day task of driving. In addition, it provides an ease of use and comfort so as to make the multitude of decisions necessary during the driving task almost automatic, and certainly effortless.

For corporate decision makers, the amount of data that must be monitored and analyzed on a given business day is anything but effortless. Hunting through spreadsheets, calling in elite information specialists, and experiencing costly delays in the synthesis process—managing information is becoming more complicated by the day. Certainly, the time has come for a new vision of the dashboard that will meet the needs of today's business professionals.

The term *dashboard* has acquired a vibrant new meaning in the field of information management as leading organizations worldwide embrace the idea of empowerment through improved real-time information systems. In the current corporate vocabulary, a *dashboard* is a rich computer interface with charts, reports, visual indicators, and alert mechanisms that are consolidated into a dynamic and relevant information platform.

Information management is a field in our new information-saturated and fast-moving business culture. Corporate America is currently abuzz with talk about enterprise performance management, balanced scorecards, business activity monitoring, and regulatory compliance. The most exciting new development in these discussions is arguably how *enterprise dashboards* can serve as live consoles to manage such business initiatives. Currently, some good books and journal papers outline the concepts and value behind various new information management initiatives, but few resources are available that fully explore the issue of *dashboard implementation.* The only available insight into the world of dashboards at this time is confined to the manuals of the software, which facilitate dashboard implementation or specialize in specific solutions with a dashboard interface. As of the writing of this book, I have found no book on the subject of enterprise dashboards. This book will shed light on the neglected subject of dashboard implementation, one that I have had the opportunity to explore, practice, and preach over the past few years.

The goal of this book is threefold:

1. *To serve as a reference and best practices guide to business leaders considering dashboards for their information needs.* C-level executives, VPs, directors, and department heads will find herein the ammunition they need to differentiate among the good, bad, and ugly of dashboarding. This book will help with due diligence for enterprise dashboarding strategy, implementation directives, and vendor selection, and will help demystify the emerging topic of dashboards.

2. *To serve as an implementation handbook for IT managers, analysts, and consultants delegated with the task of implementing dashboards.* This book provides a step-by-step implementation framework that has been tested and proven. The dashboard execution steps, storyboarding, project milestones, dashboard types, and case studies are derived from real-life implementations.

3. *To shed light on the popular topic of dashboards for teachers and students of information systems and management.* The term *dashboard* conjures an obvious image of charts and reports put together on a computer screen. Only a few minutes are required to get the basic point across. However, many variables make dashboard part science and part art. Hopefully, this book will provide enough theoretical and real-world information to prepare future information management professionals to skillfully juggle the issues involved in creating effective dashboard implementations.

The book is divided into four parts: (1) dashboard execution, (2) dashboard types, (3) dashboard software assessment, and (4) case studies.

Part One: Chapters 1 to 7 provide a framework to help readers understand the key elements of enterprise dashboards and what is involved in a dashboard implementation.

- Chapter 1 discusses the significance of dashboards in the greater context of trends in information delivery.
- Chapters 2 to 5 provide the implementation framework involving information collection, dashboard audience assessment, layout and design, and dashboard alerts.
- Chapters 6 and 7 describe the process of storyboarding and project planning with the right team composition.

Part Two: Chapters 8 and 9 provide examples for different dashboard types and implementation scenarios for various applications.

- Chapter 8 focuses on the major dashboard categories, such as the enterprise performance dashboards, activity monitoring dashboards, and customer and vendor dashboards.
- Chapter 9 focuses on divisional dashboards, such as the sales, marketing, finance, human resources, supply chain, and so forth.

Part Three: Chapters 10 and 11 provide a framework to evaluate software features and return on investment (ROI) determination.

Part Four: Chapters 12 to 14 provide real-world case studies for different types of dashboard implementations. Business managers in various organizations who have pioneered dashboard deployment in their respective business areas have contributed to these chapters to share real-world issues in dashboard implementation.

I have also borrowed notable quotes from the leaders in the information industry as well as a few of the recent management best sellers. This will help readers draw parallels between the dashboarding trend and contemporary thought from the leadership in information management.

MY BRIEF BACKGROUND

As an old-time student in the area of information management and its effect on management decisions, conceiving ways to provide improved information for decision making has always challenged me. Early in my career, after my graduate studies, I focused on data analysis, large-volume data processing, data quality, and data matching heuristics. All of these efforts are geared toward the same outcome—better information for business decision making. This quest naturally led me to the end of the tunnel, exploring information delivery to end users. Having arrived at that point, I encountered dashboards, only to discover how poor the presentation tools were for information delivery. I concluded that decision makers are data rich but information poor. The power of data analysis and number crunching has greatly advanced since then, but the average business user is inundated with *data* while seeking *information,* the proverbial needle in the haystack.

During the past few years, I have tirelessly sought to improve data visualization in order to help the average business user access the right information quickly and easily. I have championed the cause of contextual visualization, which has led to several patent-pending ideas and the development of two new product lines: iDashboards and iViz. Because dashboards fall within the space of business intelligence (BI), my quest remains to extend BI with enhanced visualization for dashboards that may be termed as *Visual Intelligence.*

WHO IS IMPLEMENTING
ENTERPRISE DASHBOARDS?

We all want to learn from the successes and failures of others. Frequently, I am asked, "Can you provide us with references of those who have implemented dashboards to address similar problems?"

During the past 12 months alone, I have had the opportunity to discuss dashboard initiatives with more than 100 organizations, ranging from Fortune 100 corporations to organizations employing 100 people. Although I'm not at liberty to divulge any names, here's a profile of some of those organizations:

- Fortune 100 automobile manufacturer
- Fortune 100 aerospace company
- Fortune 500 technology hardware and service provider

- Fortune 1000 accounting services company
- Leading real-estate information provider
- 150-year-old iron-ore mining company
- 120-year-old cash transaction services company
- Different branches of the U.S. federal government
- State and county governments
- Large and small marketing research firms
- Auto-parts distributor
- Pharmaceuticals company
- Health insurance network organization
- Financial services company
- Nonprofit fundraising organization

The list of organizations becoming involved in dashboarding continues to grow in scope and diversity. I am fortunate to have the opportunity to communicate with several organizations every week regarding their dashboarding initiatives. As diverse as the organizations are, so too are their applications of dashboards. I have seen companies implement applications including senior management dashboards, field sales reporting, dealer inventory management, supply chain management, employee scorecards, customer service level monitoring, customer information portals, marketing research, marketing and competitive intelligence, financial intelligence, regulatory compliance, and many others.

The dashboarding trend is not exclusive to the United States and Canada. Lately, I have received inquiries from South Africa, Sweden, the United Kingdom, France, Russia, China, Japan, India, Saudi Arabia, United Arab Emirates, Israel, Mexico, Brazil, Argentina, and Australia. It is clear that enterprise dashboarding is becoming a global phenomenon.

Regardless of your organizational affiliation, your location, and the applications you envision through dashboards, it is my earnest hope that this book serves as a roadmap in your drive to deliver dashboards. Bon voyage!

ACKNOWLEDGMENTS

As every author knows, there is always a team of people behind a successful endeavor of writing a book. In my case, I want to first thank my parents for their lifelong inspiration and my friends, Professor Krish Chakraborty and Quaid Saifee, for their encouragement in undertaking the idea of this book. And thanks to my wife, who facilitated my working undisturbed over many weekends stretching over a few months in the making of this book.

Furthermore, I am indebted to a team of great professionals with whom I have had the opportunity to work. I want to thank Larry Pier, *University of Michigan*, for helping me put together the illustrative dashboard screenshots, and Zaki Akmal of *iDashboards* for a similar effort. Lisa Dion of WIT did the graphic illustrations to effectively get the point across. Thanks, Lisa!

A big thank you to the team of Rhonda and Alex Reid of *Words in Motion* for editing the manuscript. They appropriately capture the spirit and limitation of many writers like me in their following prose: "There are those special people out there who have something to share with the world…people whose message carries with it a great deal of possibility. Unfortunately, these same people aren't always the kind of people who have the time or the expertise to write a book."

I am also grateful to the contributing authors who have brought in their share of real-world dashboarding experiences to this book. A special thanks to Jeff Nash of DaimlerChrysler and to Ashlee Stokes of ING DIRECT for facilitating through the case study approval process on behalf of their organizations.

Thanks to the three organizations that permitted the use of their dashboard software and sample screenshots: *Business Objects, MicroStrategy,* and *iDashboards*. And I owe a special thank you to Steve Wooledge of Business Objects for helping me champion the cause of dashboarding at various occasions.

Finally, many thanks to Sheck Cho and the team at John Wiley & Sons for steering this book through the publication process and helping me through much of its due diligence.

—**Shadan Malik**

About the Contributors

David Lewis, ING DIRECT

As the Chief Marketing and IT Officer, David oversees strategy, marketing operations, advertising, public relations, customer relationship management, alliances, IT development, IT operations, and privacy and data security at ING DIRECT USA.

Before joining ING DIRECT USA, David worked in various capacities at international banking and wealth management companies. David's educational background includes a Bachelor of Arts in Finance and Economics from the University of Western Ontario, a certificate in International Business from the University of Copenhagen, and an MBA from York University in Toronto, Canada. David is also a Chartered Financial Analyst.

Jeff Nash, DaimlerChrysler Corporation

Jeff is the Manager of Disability/Hazardous Material and Business Intelligence for DaimlerChrysler's IT and Human Resources organization. Formerly, Jeff Nash was the Manager of Business Intelligence for Global Sales and Marketing. As the business owner of Sales and Marketing's business intelligence, Jeff supported more than 1,500 field and corporate users. This responsibility included coordinating DaimlerChrysler's implementation of

Business Intelligence solutions to support Global Sales and Marketing, including the deployment of executive dashboards. *ComputerWorld* honored DaimlerChrysler with the 2004 Best Practices Award in Business Intelligence. Jeff was the business lead for the initiatives and implementation that contributed to this award.

Jonathan Rothman, Emergency Medical Associates (EMA)

Jonathan has been Director of Data Management for EMA since 1988 and has been the primary architect for EMA's data management strategies and the developer and manager of the Emergency Medicine Analysis and Reporting System (eMARS) data warehouse project, which houses clinical, operational, financial, and satisfaction data for more than 5.7 million emergency department (ED) patient encounters. EMA, a democratic physician group located in New Jersey and New York, is owned and managed by its more than 200 ED physicians and treats more than 650,000 ED patients annually.

Jonathan has spent his entire career working in health care since graduating from Temple University in 1991, with an MBA in Risk Management. His core competencies include primary group practice management, physician billing, ED operations, physician claims and financial management systems design, data warehousing, dashboard design, and business intelligence.

PART ONE

DASHBOARD EXECUTION

1

BUSINESS CASE FOR ENTERPRISE DASHBOARDS

It is a well-established management principle that you cannot manage what you cannot measure. It is equally true, however, that you cannot manage well what you cannot monitor. That is where enterprise dashboards come in.

Enterprise dashboards must provide a clear visibility to steer through the thick clouds of data overload and lack of insight.

The early years of the 21st century have seen a convergence of several management thoughts that further that age-old quest for *the right information at the right time.* The dashboard is the new face of the emerging information management field. Dashboards have become the vehicle of execution for several key initiatives being implemented among organizations worldwide. Some of those initiatives include Balanced Scorecard, Enterprise Performance Management (EPM), also referred to as Business or Corporate Performance Management (BPM), Business Activity Monitoring (BAM), Six Sigma, and the regulatory compliances such as the Sarbanes-Oxley Act.

In hindsight, dashboarding seems to reflect the natural course of progression in the quest for improved information and better decision making. Almost every organization has experienced an exponential growth in computing power and data volumes during the past years. This growth drives the organizational management to create more enlightened decision-making processes in an information-rich environment (see Exhibit 1.1).

During the past decade, capabilities for data analysis and data mining have made great strides as computing power has followed Moore's law[1] of doubling every year. However, until recently, the task of conducting power-

3

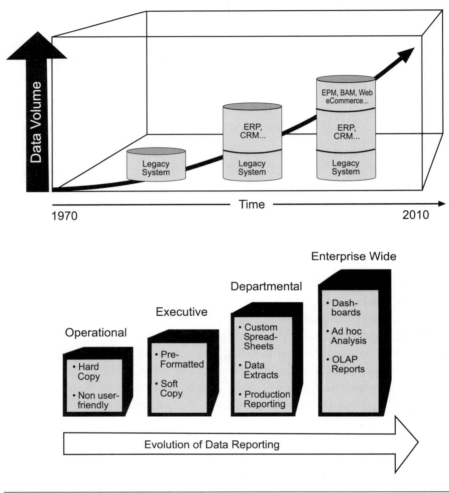

EXHIBIT 1.1   QUANTUM LEAPS IN REPORTING AND INFORMATION DELIVERY WITH THE EXPLOSIVE GROWTH IN DATA VOLUME

ful data analysis has been relegated to well-trained analysts and experts within the respective fields. The rest of the organization depended on this elite group of information champions to decide what information was dispersed, when, and in what format. If someone needed information that was not precanned, it required an ad hoc information request. By the time the requesting person received the information, it was often too late, the information was obsolete, or perhaps the need for that specific information had evaporated because of rapidly changing daily priorities. The information seeker is forced to make a gut instinct decision to quickly address the narrow window of decision making. For a business user, the frustration resulting from such delays or timely inaccessibility to information can be well imagined!

As is often the case, frustration became the mother of innovation. At first, spreadsheets became everyone's favorite tool to manipulate, store, and analyze data as they saw fit. Some departments found themselves developing databases out of Microsoft's Excel because the corporate database group or the information technology (IT) group just could not meet their information needs. In almost every organization, one can find such innovative islets of information ownership. However, information islets fall far short of meeting current needs for constantly evolving and real-time information.

As organizations open myriad fronts of interaction through their customers, vendors, and partners, they can no longer afford to handicap their front-line management with a lack of information. Anyone possessing decision-making authority that may affect organizational performance requires timely, relevant, accurate, and actionable information. Existing modes of information dispersal, whether through standardized report distribution or drag-and-drop reporting, are simply not sufficient anymore. Such reports are too static and often too overwhelming. The reader is highly susceptible to data overload. Opportunities and threats often go overlooked and are discovered too late. For these reasons, dynamic and interactive dashboards have become a fast-growing phenomena coupled with EPM and corporate compliance.

For the most part, the vendors who have developed the potential of enterprise dashboards most effectively are the reporting and Business Intelligence (BI) vendors such as Business Objects, Cognos, Hyperion, and MicroStrategy. Also, there are niche vendors such as iViz Group, iDashboards, Noetix, QPR Software, and Theoris, who have developed dashboard software with certain characteristics that have been left out by the major BI vendors.

INSPIRATION FROM AN AIRCRAFT

The dashboard within an aircraft or automobile has inspired the term *dashboard* within the information and business intelligence fields (see Exhibit 1.2). The purpose of the dashboard in all three of these settings is the same—

to monitor and drive a complex and interdependent system. David Norton and Robert Kaplan draw the analogy between an aircraft dashboard and an organizational need for similar information tools in their landmark book on the subject of Balanced Scorecards:

> Skilled pilots are able to process information from a large number of indicators to navigate their aircraft. Yet navigating today's organizations through complex competitive environments is at least as complicated as flying a jet. Why should we believe that executives need anything less than a full battery of instrumentation for guiding their companies? Managers, like pilots, need instrumentation about many aspects of their environment and performance to monitor the journey toward excellent future outcomes.[2]

If we agree that effective management of organizations requires information tools similar to those required by a pilot for flying an aircraft, we have a useful starting point to describe the basic characteristics of an organizational dashboard.

Contrary to the evident simplicity of an information dashboard, deploying an effective dashboard for a large organization is usually no less a complex task than doing the same for a jet. By no means do I mean to undermine the challenge of developing cockpit dashboards handled by aeronautical engineers, but it would be fair to assume that all aircraft dashboards display the

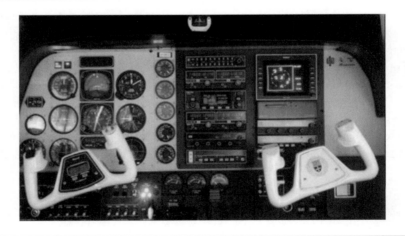

EXHIBIT 1.2   DATA PRESENTATION THROUGH A DASHBOARD, A CONCEPT DRIVEN FROM AIRCRAFT AND AUTOMOBILE TO ENTERPRISE
Source: Federal Aviation Administration Web site, www.faa.gov

same set of key performance indicators (KPIs), such as the aircraft speed, altitude, direction, wind speed, humidity, fuel status, engine temperature, latitude, longitude, and so forth. The various aircraft manufacturers may have different ergonomic designs for their dashboards, but essentially they all have to deliver to the pilots the same set of KPIs critical for a successful flight. The same applies to automotive dashboards. This leads to the ease of replication whereby an aircraft or automobile manufacturer may replicate thousands of dashboards in an assembly line to equip their aircrafts or cars, as the case may be.

However, in contrast to an aircraft or automobile, each organization has a set of KPIs that differs significantly from those of another organization. Even if two organizations are within the same industry or are close competitors, they rarely share an identical set of KPIs. Each organization's business and organizational management has evolved differently, and each division within a given organization has separate sets of KPIs relevant to itself. Finance, Supply Chain, Human Resources, Sales and Marketing— they all have their own set of KPIs that result in different types of dashboards. Although many KPIs are commonplace and standard by definition, such as gross revenue, net profit, gross margin, asset turnover ratio, and so on, each organization has unique nuances of self-management. This diversity in evolution and need necessitates conducting a thorough and individualized requirements analysis in order to build customized and effective dashboards for each organization. This provides a sharp contrast to the manufacture of thousands of cars and aircrafts with identical dashboards in an assembly-line process.

To make matters even more complex, *sources* of information that need to be presented through the enterprise dashboards are invariably in different forms within different organizations. The fact that two organizations may be using exactly the same version of a specific Enterprise Resource Planning (ERP) or Customer Relationship Management (CRM) software program alleviates the task of building these dashboards. However, no two organizations are identical in the myriad information sources that each of them would require to access for their dashboards. This makes building an enterprise dashboard a custom and complex undertaking each time.

ELEMENTS FOR AN ENTERPRISE DASHBOARD

We have borrowed inspiration from an aircraft cockpit to build enterprise dashboards, and yet we know that the analogy has some serious limitations.

So, let us establish the basic characteristics specific to an enterprise dashboard with a useful acronym—SMART. A dashboard must be SMART in that it contains the following underlying elements, which are essential for success:

Synergetic. Must be ergonomically and visually effective for a user to synergize information about different aspects within a single screen view.

Monitor KPIs. Must display critical KPIs required for effective decision making for the domain to which a dashboard caters.

Accurate. Information being presented must be entirely accurate in order to gain full user confidence in the dashboard. The supporting dashboard data must have been well tested and validated.

Responsive. Must respond to predefined thresholds by creating user alerts in addition to the visual presentation on the dashboard (e.g., sound alarms, e-mails, pagers, blinkers) to draw immediate user attention to critical matters.

Timely. Must display the most current information possible for effective decision making. The information must be *real-time* and *right-time*.

This order serves the formation of the acronym and does not indicate the relative priority of these features.

An aircraft-inspired enterprise dashboard must be SMART. However, a SMART dashboard is not sufficient to ensure effective organizational management. To the envy of pilots, an enterprise dashboard must have enhanced characteristics not available even within a cockpit. An enterprise dashboard should also have some of the following advanced elements, captured in another acronym—IMPACT:

Interactive. It should allow the user to drill down and get to details, root causes, and more. Imagine the dramatic benefit if a pilot could click on the fuel gauge showing low fuel to view the consumption rate graph during the past hour, only to find out that the consumption rate shot to twice the normal usage during the last 15 minutes, indicating a sudden fuel leak.

More data history. The dashboard should allow users to review the historical trend for a given KPI. For example, market share may indicate strength within the current time period but a negative trend in a year-ago comparison. A user may then click on the current share to investigate if a shrinking market share is a sudden phenomenon within the current time period or a trend for the past several time periods.

Personalized. The dashboard presentation should be specific to each user's domain of responsibility, privileges, data restrictions, and so on. For example, the sales manager for the Eastern region should be presented with metrics related to that region's performance and perhaps an aggregated view for other regions for relative comparison. Other aspects of personalization should be available as well, such as language and visual preferences for colors and background style, for better user experience.

Analytical. It should allow users to perform guided analysis such as what-if analysis. The dashboard should make it effortless for a user to visually navigate through different drill-down paths, compare, contrast, and make analytical inferences. In this way, the dashboard can facilitate better business comprehension within a set of interdependent business variables.

Collaborative. The dashboard should facilitate users' ability to exchange notes regarding specific observations on their dashboards. This could also be adopted to accomplish workflow checks and process controls. A well-designed collaboration would serve as a communication platform for task management and compliance control.

Trackability. It should allow each user to customize the metrics he or she would like to track. Such customized tracking could then be incorporated within the default dashboard view presented to the user after login. For example, the sales managers for the Eastern and Western regions may not want to track the same issues. The Eastern region may be facing a highly competitive pressure with a low market share, whereas the Western region may have a high market share but an inventory problem leading to out-of-stock situations.

Again, this order does not indicate the relative priority of these features, but it provides another acronym to remember easily—IMPACT. Therefore, an organizational dashboard must have SMART IMPACT.

RULES OF GOOD SOFTWARE STILL APPLY

Having laid the foundation for an effective organizational dashboard, it is worth noting that the dashboard software must also meet the standards of any good software, which include the following:

- *Fast response.* Users should not experience an inordinate delay in retrieving their dashboards and associated reports.

- *Intuitive.* End users need not be required to go through a big learning curve or mandatory training.

- *Web-based.* Users should be able to access the dashboard through the Web, if they have proper access rights. The Web-based feature may also be referred to as *thin client.*

- *Secured.* System administrators may administer software security easily to reduce and track wrongful access. The software must also provide data encryption to secure sensitive data transmission across the Web.

- *Scalable.* A large number of users may access the software without crashing the system or causing it to slow down below an acceptable performance benchmark. This quality assumes a reasonable hardware and network bandwidth.

- *Industry compliant.* The software should integrate with standard databases of different vendors and work with different server standards (e.g., Net, J2EE) and various operating systems (e.g., Unix, Windows, Linux).

- *Open technology.* The software should not have proprietary standards that would make it difficult or impossible to extend its reach within a complex IT environment. It should work well with the prevailing protocols for information exchange, such as the XML, ODBC, JDBC, OLE DB, JMS, and Web Services. Note, open technology does not mean *open source,* which refers mostly to free software with open access to the source code.

- *Supportable.* It should be easy to manage a large deployment within the existing IT staff with limited training on the dashboard software. In other words, the software should not be so complex that it requires long-term contract or hiring of another expert simply to support its deployment, assuming that the organization has a reasonably qualified IT staff.

- *Cost effective.* The total cost of ownership should be well below the monetary benefit it provides to justify a strong return on investment (ROI). Therefore, the licensing cost, implementation cost, and support cost should be within a range that provides strong ROI and organizational benefits after deployment.

COMMON MISPERCEPTIONS ABOUT DASHBOARDS

There are certain perceptions about enterprise dashboards that are simply wrong.

Dashboards Are for Senior Executives Only (Wrong!)

A commonly prevalent notion is that enterprise dashboards are *only* for senior executives to give them an overall view of organizational performance. Not true! Today's dashboard technology is designed to make an enterprise dashboard an effective tool to be deployed at various levels within the organization.

Most companies deploying dashboards have rolled them out to thousands of members of their workforce. In some cases, organizations initiate by rolling dashboards out to a small group of people, often the senior executives, but invariably the vision has been to deploy it organization-wide once the concept is well tested and proven.

A rule of thumb should be that if anyone in the organization is responsible for managing $1 million or more per year in direct business or internal resources, that staff member should be provided with an appropriate dashboard to help increase productivity. The math is simple: If the dashboard improves productivity and revenue for a 1% gain, then the return is at a minimum $10,000 per year for the individual. An enterprise-wide deployment and support of dashboards should cost a fraction of this, and hence have a strong ROI.

The following are the contemporary thoughts of industry leaders within the business intelligence space:

> We honestly believe that the BI of the past was really designed for a subset of users in an enterprise who understood deep analytics, the PhDs in analytics. But our view is you can't solve business problems unless we move [BI] closer to the user, and that is where our investments are going.
> —Karen Parrish, VP of BI Solutions, IBM[3]

> In 5 years, BI will be as ubiquitous as spreadsheet and word processing today.
> —Bernard Liautaud, Chairman and CEO, Business Objects[4]

As visionaries and business intelligence (BI) industry leaders predict such ubiquity of BI, dashboards would be just as ubiquitous as the new face of BI.

Dashboards Are for Report Distribution Only (Wrong!)

Dashboard deployment should not be treated only as a platform for convenient report distribution and KPI viewing. This greatly diminishes the true value and effectiveness of dashboards and how they can enhance organizational performance. Imagine that a car's dashboard displayed a detailed report on how much gas was filled during the current month, instead of sounding a visual and audio alarm to the driver when the car is running low on gas. The report would not be of much use in this instance, because the key quality of real-time functionality would be lost.

Although it does so much more, the *central* purpose of a dashboard is to warn the user when any relevant metrics are out of acceptable boundaries. In the dashboard terminology, these *alerts* consisting of rules and actions add critical value to an enterprise dashboard deployment complemented with strong visual indicators of warnings.

DEFINITIONS FOR FUTURE REFERENCE

You should now have a familiar understanding of the scope and functionality of enterprise dashboards for organizations through comparison and contrast with aircraft and automotive dashboards. Now we leave the aircraft and automobile behind. In subsequent chapters, all references to the term dashboard will refer to the *enterprise dashboard*. (Others may use the terms corporate dashboard, executive dashboard, and so on, but the meaning is the same.)

DIFFERENCE BETWEEN PORTAL AND DASHBOARD

The distinguishing feature is that a dashboard is an application with a collection of metrics, benchmarks, goals, results, and alerts presented in a visually effective manner, whereas a portal is a collection of different applications presented together within a personalized framework. A dashboard could be part of a portal, but not vice versa.

A portal, for example, could contain a dashboard, a company's events calendar, weather conditions, individual profile details, financial market conditions, financial stock tracking, and so on. A dashboard in its strictest definition should not contain a company's events calendar, personalized weather conditions, and other elements like these. There are dedicated portals for varied applications such as e-commerce, auctions, e-mails, as well as corporate portals for company information. A dashboard, however, is intended specifically for the presentation of organizational and individual performance metrics and alerts.

Metrics

Metrics are measurements of activities to evaluate performance, mostly within a relative framework of time, geography, and aggregation. For example, a sales metric may be *Gross Sales for Quarter 1 for North America for an Item/Category*.

Enterprise Performance Management and Business Intelligence

EPM is the application of BI, metrics, and methodologies to improve enterprise performance. BI is the capability to track, understand, and manage information across the organization.

ENDNOTES

1. Gordon Moore, co-founder of Intel, observed in 1965 that since the invention of the integrated circuit, the number of transistors per square inch on integrated circuits had doubled every year. Mr. Moore predicted that this trend would continue for the foreseeable future. In subsequent years, the pace slowed down a bit, but data density has doubled approximately every 18 months, and this is the current definition of Moore's Law.
2. Robert S. Kaplan and David P. Norton, *The Balanced Scorecard: Translating Strategy into Action* (Boston: Harvard Business School Press, 1996), p. 2.
3. Ed Scannell, "IBM Rolls Out BI Solution for Banks," *InfoWorld*, March 15, 2004.
4. Bernard Liautaud, Chairman and CEO, Business Objects, *Business Objects Americas Partner Summit keynote speech*, Palm Springs, California, May 18, 2004.

2

DASHBOARDING PROCESS

The Meta-Information

1. What information?
2. For whom?
3. How to present?

The entire dashboarding process could be mapped along the answers to the previous three questions. This chapter addresses the first question, and the subsequent two chapters address the second and third questions.

WHAT INFORMATION?

Meta-information is information about information. For those from the information technology (IT) or database profession, this would resonate with the concept of *metadata*—data about data.

Dashboard implementation at the level of meta-information requires collecting information about the information required to display through dashboards. On a primary level, this process involves determining the critical business questions that need to be answered through dashboard deployment, and then mapping these questions to the key performance indicators (KPIs) that need to be captured through the dashboards in order to get answers and insight.

The first step in this process is to document all of the KPIs that are currently being captured through regular reports or ad hoc analysis. Usually, such KPIs are well documented and mapped to the various data sources required to generate them. At this stage, it would also be useful to determine if any KPIs are desired by decision makers but for some reason are not currently made available.

Another strategy for thorough cataloging of KPIs is to divide them by various divisions within the organization (e.g., Sales, Marketing, Manufacturing, Supply Chain, Customer Service, Human Resources, Finance). It is very likely that at any given time, a dashboarding effort deals with a single division, and therefore, for the most part, the necessary KPIs are relevant to that specific division only. However, eventually the needs of the organization will require that dashboards within one division tap into KPIs from other divisions in order to build an understanding of the big picture. Senior executive dashboards would invariably require consolidation of KPIs from all divisions.

The following are some standard KPIs for various divisions:

- *Sales KPIs*. Gross and Net Revenue, Unit Sales, Number of Orders, Average Order Value, Pipeline Conversion Rate, Active Forecast, Days Since Last Sale, Revenue per Employee

- *Marketing KPIs*. Percentage of Promotion Response, Price Elasticity, Unique Web Site Visits, Product Sales Mix

- *Supply chain KPIs*. Cycle Time, Stock Quantity, Lost Sales Volume, Return Rate, On-Time Delivery Percentage, Inventory Turn

- *Customer service KPIs*. Retention Percentage, Cross-Sold Percentage, Service Level Met Percentage, Handling Time, Call Time, First-Time Resolution Percentage, Referral Percentage, Unresolved Percentage, Case Aging

- *Human resources KPIs*. Headcount, Employee Turnover Ratio, Average Tenure Length, Hire Cycle Time, Skill Level

- *Finance KPIs*. Revenue, Gross Profit, Gross Margin Percentage, Net Income, Accounts Receivable, Cash Flow, Asset Turnover Ratio, Cash Flow

- *Manufacturing KPIs*. Labor as a Percentage of Cost, Downtime Percentage, Variance from Plan, Time from Order to Shipment, Time on Floor to Be Packed

These KPIs will be explored in greater depth in Chapter 9 on divisional dashboards.

DEFINING THE KEY PERFORMANCE INDICATORS

The process of defining the KPIs for dashboards is no different than doing the same for building a reporting infrastructure (or business intelligence system). To perform this process with full rigor and detail, an experienced information analyst is required. This person must acquire a thorough knowledge of the disparate information sources within the organization and the existing business intelligence infrastructure, and gain a fair understanding of the business processes along with the information requirements. Also, that analyst needs to be able to tap into a team of subject matter experts from business divisions, IT, and data analytics to complete a full picture.

Each KPI should be broken down into four elements:

1. Data source(s)
2. Granularity
3. Calculation
4. Variance

These elements together define the full scope and illuminate the different facets of a particular KPI. Information pertaining to each of these elements needs to be compiled in order to get a clear picture for each KPI (see Exhibit 2.1). The following sections describe in detail each of the elements.

Data Sources

Data sources would identify the high-level information regarding where to retrieve the information for a given KPI. Such high-level information includes database identification (specific data mart or data warehouse), Online Analytical Processing (OLAP) sources (specific cubes), data files (extract from legacy systems or data from external vendors), or existing reports and supporting sources (such as universes and objects). Exhibit 2.2 illustrates a typical medley of data sources within a large organization that I refer to as the *information biosphere*. There are inherent challenges in integrating the myriad sources so that they seamlessly communicate with dashboard software to present all information in complete harmony.

During the process of identifying all of the KPI data sources within the information biosphere, loopholes that may exist within the organization's information delivery process may surface. For example, the process may reveal a lack of standards, lack of data validation, and data redundancies across var-

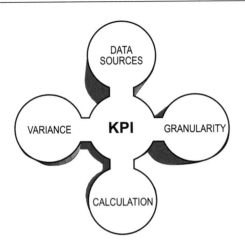

EXHIBIT 2.1 THE FOUR ELEMENTS OF A KPI

ious data sources. Therefore, it is a recurring phenomenon that the process of defining KPIs spawns a parallel effort into standardization, data mart development, data warehouse enhancement, and extraction, transformation, and loading (ETL) procedures. In other words, the process often initiates a full tune-up with overall checks and balances for maintaining a sustainable and balanced information biosphere within the organization.

Because the dashboard's function is to report on all aspects within the information biosphere, it is essential that the dashboard software have appropriate *sensors* to communicate with the different information sources. In the IT community, such sensors are referred to as database drivers, application programming interfaces (APIs), agents, adapters, and so on.

A comprehensive sensor checkup for the dashboard software would lead to a gap analysis between requirements and the capabilities of the software. In other words, if data sources include different relational databases, OLAP cubes, a vendor-specific reporting platform, and a vendor-specific Enterprise Resource Planning (ERP) system, it is imperative that the dashboard software be capable of communicating with all of these disparate sources. If the dashboard software falls short in connecting to a vendor-specific reporting platform, then an alternative is required to transform the information from its original platform into a more standard data representation that is readable by the dashboard software.

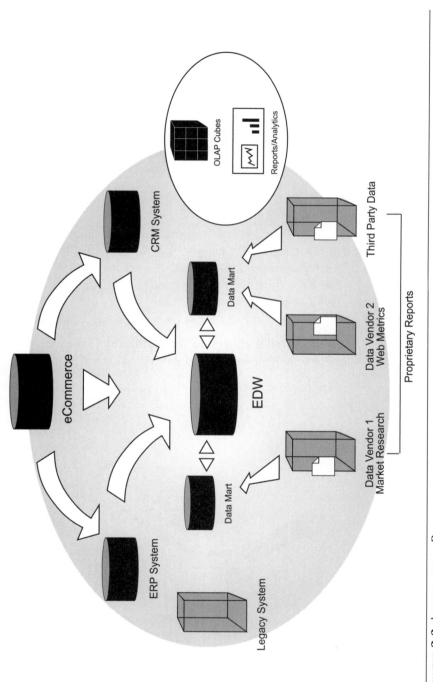

EXHIBIT 2.2 INFORMATION BIOSPHERE

19

It is also important to note that a single KPI may involve multiple data sources. For example, determining the market share of a company's product may require the sales data from the enterprise data warehouse (EDW), and the total sale within that category as reported by an external vendor tracking the industry, reported through that vendor's proprietary reporting interface. If the vendor uses a proprietary homegrown reporting system, most likely any standard dashboard software would not be able to extract data from such reports. Therefore, dashboarding requires additional efforts to consolidate disparate data sources into a seamless data communication platform. This I refer to as the *harmonization of the information biosphere.*

Granularity

Granularity establishes the various levels of calculations required for each of the KPIs. Each KPI could have different grains across the three basic dimensions: (1) time, (2) geography, and (3) product. All unique and feasible combinations across the three dimensions determine the different grains of an individual KPI (see Exhibit 2.3).

Time grain determines the time attributes for a given KPI, such as hourly, daily, weekly, monthly, quarterly, yearly, year-to-date, and so on. *Geography grain* determines the geographic area attributes, such as world, region, country, state, section, territory, city, zip code, outlet type, and so on. Finally, *product grain* determines the product grouping attributes, such as company total, division, product category, brand, item group, item, Universal Product

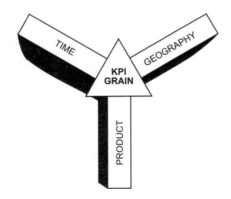

Exhibit 2.3 Three Basic Dimensions that Determine the Grain of a KPI

Code (UPC), and so on. Note that service groupings could also be represented within this dimension, as illustrated in the following examples.

Note that Example 1 shows how the different automotive categories and a brand manufactured by the company are the different grains of the product dimension. The geography dimension includes the Worldwide, USA, and East Region within the USA.

Example 1. A Multinational Automotive Company

Gross Revenue (GR): A very common KPI that is required across every granular combination of the three basic dimensions within an organization. Some possible grains for this KPI are:

KPI	Time	Geography	Product
GR	YTD (Year-to-Date)	Worldwide	Company Total
GR	Current Month	Worldwide	Company Total
GR	Latest Week	Worldwide	Company Total
GR	YTD	USA	Company Total
GR	YTD	USA	SUVs Total
GR	YTD	USA	Trucks Total
GR	YTD	USA	Cars Total
GR	YTD	USA–East	Trucks Total
GR	YTD	USA–East	Cars Total
GR	YTD	USA–East	Brand Series 3 Total
GR	YTD	USA–East	Brand Series 5 Total

Note that Example 2 shows the different areas of customer service provided by the company as different grains of the product dimension. The geography dimension has the total US, East Region, New York (NY) state, and New York City's metropolitan area. Geography could be extended to individual customers, such as specific corporate accounts and their regions.

Example 2: A Customer Service Organization within the United States

Percent Resolution (% Res): The percentage of complaints resolved through customer service personnel, a critical KPI required across all granularity within the business. Some KPI grains are as follows:

KPI	Time	Geography	Product
%Res	YTD	USA	Company Total
%Res	Current Month	USA	Company Total
%Res	Latest Week	USA	Company Total
%Res	YTD	USA–East	Server Support
%Res	YTD	USA–East	Laptop Support
%Res	YTD	USA–East	PC Support
%Res	YTD	USA–NY	Server Support
%Res	YTD	USA–NY	Laptop Support
%Res	YTD	USA–NY	PC Support
%Res	YTD	NY–NY City	Server Support
%Res	YTD	NY–NY City	Laptop Support
%Res	YTD	NY–NY City	PC Support

Note that unlike Example 1, this KPI would carry limited grains only and will not have a Worldwide geographic grain or Latest Week time grain. The reason is that Worldwide or weekly sales data for the company vehicles may not have the corresponding industry sales data, which is available only for North America at a monthly level. This is a hypothetical example, which illustrates varying levels of granularity among different KPIs.

The total grains for a KPI could quickly add up in volume if each of the three granular dimensions has a large set of values. Therefore, an accurate assessment of all grains for each KPI is important in order to derive a good estimate of the total data elements required to be delivered through the dashboards. Such an assessment also helps in building an effective navigation and user experience through appropriate drill-down paths.

Example 3: A Multinational Automotive Company

Market Share (MSh): A critical KPI that is determined based on industry data available by a data vendor, which provides data only for monthly, quarterly, and yearly aggregates within North America. Some possible grains are as follows:

KPI	Time	Geography	Product
MSh	Latest Qtr	USA	Company Total
MSh	Latest Qtr	Canada	Company Total
MSh	Latest Qtr	USA	Trucks Total
MSh	Latest Qtr	USA	Cars Total
MSh	Latest Qtr	USA–East	Trucks Total
MSh	Latest Qtr	USA–East	Cars Total

Calculation

Calculation would indicate any mathematical operation required to arrive at a given KPI. If a KPI is extracted from a single data source, then in most cases it requires appropriate data joins to aggregate the correct data.

The most often used calculations to arrive at a KPI from a single data source are sum, average, and percentage. However, depending on the situation, other statistical functions, such as minimum, maximum, moving average, weighted average, and so on, are also utilized. If a KPI is extracted from two or more data sources, calculations may involve complex joins across the data sources with conditional computations.

The following are some examples of a few popular KPI calculations from a single data source:

- Revenue: Sum of revenue
- Gross Profit (Loss) %: (Sum of Revenue − Sum of Cost) × 100 ÷ Sum of Revenue
- Percent Resolution: (Sum of all successful resolutions) × 100 ÷ (Sum of all customer calls)
- 12-month Moving Average Revenue: (Sum of Revenue for current 12 months) ÷ 12

Calculation also indicates the aggregation characteristics of a KPI. Depending on the calculation, it may or may not be possible to roll up the lower grains of a KPI to arrive at the higher aggregated grains. For instance, in the previous examples, Revenue is the only KPI that may be aggregated by rolling up the lower grains. Gross Profit Percentage, Percent Resolution, and Monthly Moving Average Revenue cannot be simply rolled up from lower-grain data. Such nonaggregate KPIs must be precomputed for each granular level, whereas aggregate KPIs could have greater flexibility for on-the-fly rollups from lower-grain data. These details are important in building the navigational path and personalized dashboards at different granular levels and in building the supporting data elements for such dashboard deployments.

For example, consider the building of a dashboard to deploy across 1,200 geographic grains organized at five levels: (1) Continents, (2) Country, (3) Country-Region, (4) State, and (5) Territory. Each geographic unit has a manager responsible for that geography. The product grain has a product line with 50 items organized into four levels of groupings: (1) Company, (2) Brand, (3) Category, and (4) Item Totals. If a dashboard solution were designed such that each manager gets a personalized dashboard with the aforementioned four KPIs relevant to the corresponding geography organized by product, the due diligence on KPIs' granularity and calculation would be essential.

Variance

Variance establishes the comparison benchmark for each KPI. It has two requirements: (1) the basis for change and (2) change calculation. The most commonly applied references for the basis are relative periodic comparisons: year ago, quarter ago, and month ago. Other types of change basis are forecast, operational plan, quota, and so on. The most commonly applied values for change calculations are Difference, Percentage Change, and Percent Point Change.

Some typical examples of KPI variances are as follows:

- Percentage change in Revenue for the same period a year ago (YAGO). Change calculation is defined as (Current Value − YAGO Value) × 100 ÷ YAGO Value.

- Point change in Market Share from the previous quarter. Change calculation is defined as (Current Market Share − Previous Quarter's Market Share).

To establish a uniform performance benchmark across the organization, it is important that variance of a specific KPI be consistent across all of its possible grains. Therefore, in the earlier example, change in revenue across all geographies, brands, and time periods would always be calculated as a percentage change for the same time a year ago for corresponding geographies and brands.

Note that a single KPI could require multiple variance calculations. For example, it may be required that the revenue also reflects Quarter Ago Percentage Change and Month Ago Difference. KPIs' variance plays a key role in defining business rules to configure alerts and triggers for dashboards.

See Exhibit 2.4 for a framework that would help consolidate all of the relevant details behind the four elements required of the KPIs.

KPI	Data Source				Granularity		
Name	Report	Universe/Cube	Database	Other	Time	Geography	Product

Calculation		Variance		Threshold			Alert	
Formula	Additive	Basis	Calculation	Lower	Middle	Upper	Action	Recipient(s)

EXHIBIT 2.4 FRAMEWORK TO MAP THE KPI DETAILS REQUIRED FOR BUILDING DASHBOARDS

DEFINING THE KPI THRESHOLDS

KPI thresholds are parameters set by the organization in order to evaluate performance and organize action around the flow of information. These thresholds are the units of information that allow dashboards to perform as monitors for Enterprise Performance Management (EPM) and Business Activity Monitoring (BAM).

Knowing the values of a KPI and the variances related to it still does not give us the final business bottom line that is needed. Is it good, bad, or just okay? Defining the KPI thresholds will complete the picture and help the organization obtain those vital qualitative answers.

KPI thresholds may vary for each of the KPI grains, and they are established and owned by the respective domain managers to which a KPI grain belongs. However, often a corporate benchmark may be set that would apply within the organization across all grains for a given KPI. For example, a company may decide that revenue changes would have the following thresholds:

- Excellent   Over 10% increase for YTD against a year ago
- Good   5% to 10% increase for YTD against a year ago
- Okay   0% to 5% increase for YTD against a year ago
- Poor   Up to 5% decrease for YTD against a year ago
- Extremely Poor   Over 5% decrease for YTD against a year ago

Note that in the previous example, the thresholds for the revenue change may apply uniformly across all geography and product grains.

However, in some cases, this may not hold true. For example, considering the case of Percentage Resolution for customer service, different thresholds may apply for different product groups. An organization may define the thresholds as follows:

For Business Accounts
- Excellent   Over 90% Resolution for Latest Month
- Good   80% to 90% Resolution for Latest Month
- Okay   75% to 80% Resolution for Latest Month
- Poor   Below 75% Resolution for Latest Month

For Consumer Accounts
- Excellent   Over 80% Resolution for Latest Month
- Good   70% to 80% Resolution for Latest Month

- Okay   60% to 70% Resolution for Latest Month
- Poor   Below 60% Resolution for Latest Month

Note that in the previous example, thresholds are set directly on the KPIs and not on the variance. Second, the thresholds are different for the same KPI (Percentage Resolution) for different product grains—business accounts versus consumer accounts. The company may want to place higher priority on attending to calls from business accounts, or it may have more technicians attending to business accounts as compared to consumer accounts.

Similarly, different geography or time grains may have different thresholds for the same KPI. Typical reasons for variance in thresholds by geographic regions could be staffing, distance, or regional competition. The usual reason for variance in thresholds by length of time periods is that shorter time periods carry factors lending to higher volatility as compared to longer periods.

It is also a better practice from the point of managing large deployments to have thresholds as percentage change. Such thresholds can be more easily applied across most grains as compared to actual difference. Depending on the KPIs' expected value for each grain, the threshold must change if it is based on actual difference.

For example, if thresholds were designed against revenue differences, for each time period, for each product group, and for each geographic region, they would be potentially different. This would eliminate the ability to set enterprise-wide benchmarks against which all grains could be measured uniformly.

Consider a company-level threshold for monthly revenue versus a year ago that is defined as follows:

- Excellent   Over $1 million increase
- Good $500,000 to $1 million increase
- Okay $0 to $500,000 increase
- Poor   Any decrease

These threshold definitions would not be applicable for assessing quarterly or yearly revenue, and they would not apply toward individual product grains or geographic regions within the organization, each of which have a much smaller revenue base compared to the overall organization.

Despite these challenges, at times a well-rounded performance evaluation system may require thresholds against absolute differences in the KPI values. However, such thresholds should be restricted to limited grains within the KPI, or ongoing maintenance of such thresholds against a large organization-wide deployment may be counterproductive and prone to error.

EXHIBIT 2.5 SPEEDOMETER DISPLAYING DIFFERENT THRESHOLDS

A popular graphic format to visualize thresholds and relative performance is a speedometer (or dial). The color bands within the speedometer represent the different threshold levels, and the needle represents the actual data value (see Exhibit 2.5). Another graphic representation of relative performance against thresholds is a circular image (popularly referred to as *traffic light*), the color of which indicates relative performance.

DEFINING THE ALERTS

Alerts and KPI thresholds are two sides of the same coin. Alerts are actions taken once a KPI threshold is reached. However, alerts are not defined for every threshold boundary. For the most part, they serve as a warning system when a KPI shows poor performance or an undesired trend (see Exhibit 2.6). Alerts must always be accompanied by attention-capturing actions such as automatic e-mails and/or visual indication such as blinking or animation on the dashboard. The other variable for alerts is the recipient. There may be one or more appropriate recipients for each alert.

Alerts function to promote *management by exception*. With the ever-growing information load, it is possible that a user may overlook a red flag in a KPI. However, alerts assure that any negative exception is not overlooked and that appropriate personnel are informed immediately.

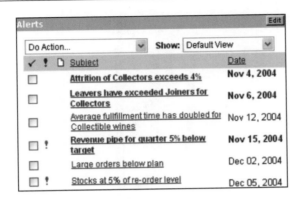

EXHIBIT 2.6 ALERTS SHOWN ON A USER SCREEN WHEN KPI THRESHOLDS EXCEED DEFINED PARAMETERS

In addition to dispersing the information to the right person at the right time, alerts may also be deployed to introduce system-controlled checks and balances and to institute appropriate actions or events. For example, if inventory level goes below the minimum threshold for a certain part, an alert may trigger a purchase order in the system for a preset quantity against the supplier of that part. To ensure human validation, the alert must also create an information trail to inform the responsible individual(s). In other words, alerts must have the capability to undertake multiple actions, some of which could be system events.

Any sophisticated ERP system would usually have such system-generated alerts for inventory levels. However, dashboards may be deployed in many business processes that are not managed by an ERP system. There is a growing trend to manage customer attrition, fraud, on-demand computing, and so on, through Business Activity Monitoring. A dashboard with a strong alert system would serve well toward effective management of these processes. A much more in-depth discussion on the topic of dashboard alerts follows in Chapter 5.

DEFINING HIERARCHIES

Hierarchies are company-specific structures for rollups that correspond to the organizational management. Each of the three dimensions of granularity (i.e., time, geography, and product) has its own hierarchy (see Exhibit 2.7). The following are some examples of hierarchies:

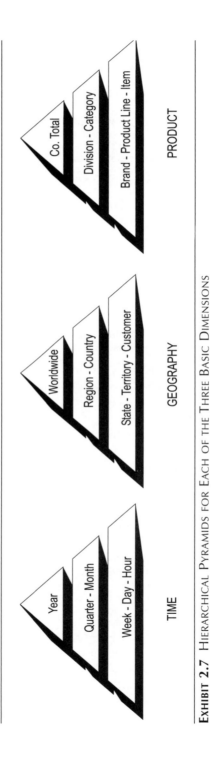

EXHIBIT 2.7 HIERARCHICAL PYRAMIDS FOR EACH OF THE THREE BASIC DIMENSIONS

- *Time.* Year, Quarter, Month, Day
- *Geography.* Worldwide, Region, Country, State, City, Zip, Customer
- *Product.* Company, Category, Brand, Item

Often, an organization will have multiple hierarchies for the same granular dimension. For example, Finance and Accounting may require a time hierarchy of year—quarter—month, whereas Operations may have no relevance for month because they manage by week and days. So, they may require a time hierarchy of year—quarter—week—day. Similarly, different areas within a large organization may look at geographic hierarchy in different ways depending on what best relates to their management process. Exhibits 2.8 and 2.9 illustrate examples of parallel hierarchies within the geography and product dimensions, respectively.

Two areas in the dashboarding process are affected by hierarchies:

1. Dashboard layout and navigation
2. User profiling and customization

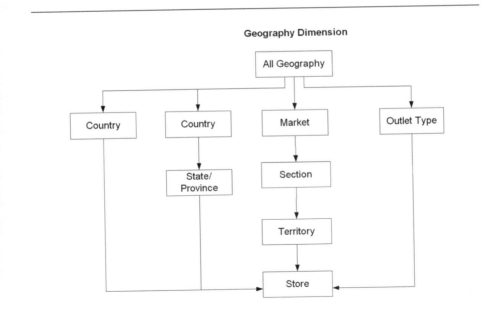

EXHIBIT 2.8 MULTIPLE HIERARCHIES WITHIN THE GEOGRAPHY DIMENSION

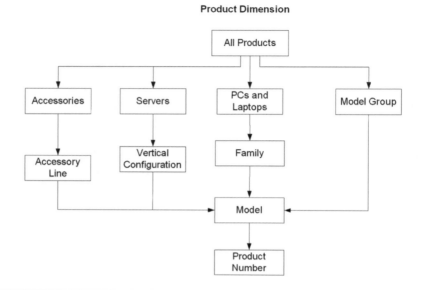

EXHIBIT 2.9 MULTIPLE HIERARCHIES WITHIN THE PRODUCT DIMENSION

Before determining the dashboard layout and organization of menus, it is important to understand the hierarchical relationship among the various grains within each granular dimension. For example, if a dashboard has a navigational menu, how should this menu be built to meaningfully represent the particular business structure? Each item on the menu may represent a geographic region, and clicking on the menu item may expand into submenus that have the product hierarchy for that region.

Another aspect of dashboard navigation is determining the drill-down paths. If a dashboard displays a chart showing monthly revenue, what would a user see if that chart is clicked or a specific point on that chart is clicked? More on this topic is covered in Chapter 4, but suffice it to say that hierarchy definitions are key in determining navigational paths and resulting user experience within the dashboard.

User profiling helps present the most relevant information to the user. For example, a territory manager needs to be presented with all relevant KPIs for the territory. Two factors play into the profiling process: user privilege and relevance.

In many cases, a company's security policy would not permit the territory manager to see data for any other territory or region. Information security is managed by establishing and assigning appropriate privileges for each user. (More about this process will follow in Chapter 3.)

Even if there is not a security restriction, it is important to determine the user relevance and provide the easiest access to the information that is most relevant to each user. For example, a territory manager will be most concerned with his or her own territory, so that data must be displayed first. However, that manager may benefit from access to information regarding other territories or regions, and this information must be accessible as well.

Therefore, to present a customized dashboard based on user profile, it is important to know the hierarchy node and dimensional grains at that node applicable to a given user profile. For example, if a customer service accounts manager is responsible for corporate accounts in the metro New York area, the dashboard architecture should be designed so that KPIs applicable to this granular cross-section are presented to that user.

3

THE AUDIENCE

BI is moving from the boardroom to the mailroom, to the factory floor.
—Bernard Liautaud, Chairman and CEO, Business Objects[1]

Chapter 2 provided an overview of the issues involved in answering the question: *What information?* This chapter addresses the second relevant question for the dashboarding process: *For whom?*

Audience is a key design factor within the dashboarding architecture. Determining user profiles and their privilege domains will contribute to the creation of a personalized dashboard experience. An effective dashboard must only present those KPIs that are relevant to a given user and within the user's domain of privilege. These KPIs must also reflect the specific grains relevant to the user.

Dashboard personalization requires the establishment of a three-dimensional framework (see Exhibit 3.1) inclusive of the following:

1. User groups and hierarchies
2. Privilege domain
3. Content domain

USER GROUPS AND HIERARCHIES

The main purpose for developing user groups and hierarchies is to avoid the repetitive task of allocating certain sets of privilege and content access to each individual user. Establishing such groupings allows allocating a set of privileges to all users within a given group with a single stroke of software

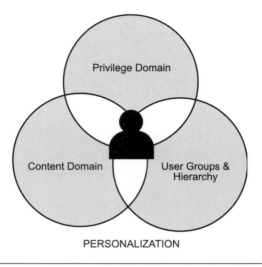

PERSONALIZATION

EXHIBIT 3.1 DASHBOARD PERSONALIZATION IS AN INTERSECTION OF A THREE-
DIMENSIONAL FRAMEWORK

command. Similarly, through inheritance, multiple user groups within the
hierarchy may be allocated a set of privileges with a single click.

For example, if 500 sales personnel require access to reports with sales
trend, market share, and sales forecast variance, this could be accomplished
in a single stroke by grouping these 500 people as the Sales Group and giving this group access to corresponding KPIs and reports common to them all.
However, in a more realistic situation, 50 of these sales personnel may be
responsible for only one of ten regions, say Region 1. Additionally, 20 customer service reps and 25 distribution personnel may be assigned to Region
1, all of them requiring competitive market share information in Region 1. In
this case, a hierarchy for Region 1 would include sales, customer service,
and distribution groups to inherit the same set of reports or KPIs. Note that
there would be separate groups such as Region 1 Sales, Region 1 Customer
Service, and Region 1 Distribution because each of them may need a separate set of KPIs unique to each group, while also requiring a certain common
set of KPIs for Region 1.

The example in Exhibit 3.2 is a simplified scenario to illustrate the role
of groups and hierarchies in the dashboarding process. Such groups and hierarchies are determined based on business requirements and information
needs. User hierarchies may be multilevel, which allows a cascading of priv-

ilege sets from higher to lower levels. A user may belong to more than one group, and therefore inherit a combination of privileges from all of the groups to which he or she belongs. In Exhibit 3.2, users in the Region 1 Sales group inherit privileges from Region 1 and Sales hierarchies.

Over the years, applications of user groups and hierarchies have been most prevalent within the different database management and business intelligence software. Any experienced database administrator can help build an effective user hierarchy and groups if the organization does not already have a matured business intelligence (BI) infrastructure in place. However, user groups and hierarchies in a database context are rarely helpful in managing a dashboard deployment because those groups and hierarchies enforce the access privilege to database resources—tables, views, columns, and database commands—whereas the dashboard groups enforce the restrictions and privileges related to dashboards functions, features, and KPIs, which are very different than a database.

However, if there already exists an enterprise-wide reporting system, most likely its user groups and hierarchies could well serve as the frame-

+ Region 1	
- Region 1 Sales	(100 users)
- Region 1 CS	(20 users)
- Region 1 Dist	(25 users)
+ Region 2	
- Region 2 Sales	(80 users)
- Region 2 CS	(15 users)
- Region 2 Dist	(20 users)
+ Region 3	
- Region 3 Sales	(75 users)
- Region 3 CS	(12 users)
- Region 3 Dist	(16 users)
+ Sales	
- Region 1 Sales	(100 users)
- Region 2 Sales	(80 users)
- Region 3 Sales	(75 users)

CS–Customer Service; Dist–Distribution

EXHIBIT 3.2 A SINGLE-LEVEL HIERARCHY EXAMPLE WITH MULTIPLE USER GROUPS

work for dashboard deployments. User groups and hierarchies in a report-distribution system cater to the information needs of users in accordance with the business needs. This logic is similar to the framework of a dashboard deployment. Therefore, BI vendors commonly have their dashboard software tightly integrated to the user management module within their reporting software. This also reduces the burden of administering user groups and privileges.

Before starting to develop user groups and hierarchies for a dashboard deployment, one needs to acquire a clear understanding of the separate business functions and their varying information needs. It is important to know the organizational hierarchy, the domain of responsibility defined for each level of hierarchy, and the corresponding information needs. This information is essential in building a dashboard framework that encompasses both privilege and content domains.

PRIVILEGE DOMAIN

A privilege denotes one or more functions that may be performed within the software. Typically, some of the privileges (functions) within a dashboard environment would be the following:

- Create a new dashboard for individual viewing only
- Create a new dashboard for all users' viewing
- Modify an existing dashboard
- Post a communication on a collaborative dashboard
- Create underlying elements for a dashboard such as KPIs, alerts, reports, charts, and dashboard templates
- Create a category or a navigation tab for grouping of dashboards
- Create a dashboard user
- Change the user privilege of an existing user
- Define a new privilege
- Define user groups and hierarchies
- Determine dashboard refresh frequency
- Define a new database or data source connection

These privileges are essentially functions that may be performed within a dashboard software program. Therefore, privilege is simply a software function, and each privilege domain is a unique collection of those functions.

Often, a set of privileges is collectively referred to as a *role*. For example, the previous list of privileges could be grouped into three sets and each set associated to a role. The three roles and the corresponding set of privileges could be:

Business User Role
- Create a new dashboard for individual viewing only
- Post a communication on a collaborative dashboard

Power User or Analyst Role
- Create a new dashboard for individual viewing only
- Create a new dashboard for other users' viewing
- Modify an existing dashboard
- Post a communication on a collaborative dashboard
- Create underlying elements for a dashboard such as KPIs, alerts, reports, charts, and dashboard templates
- Create a category or a navigation tab for grouping of dashboards

Administrator Role
- All of the dashboard functions permitted within the dashboard software

Note that roles help to easily manage a large user base in that a role assignment to a user group provides all of the users within that group with a corresponding set of dashboard privileges. However, it is possible that some software may not have roles, and instead will simply have a set of functions that may be allocated or revoked to individual users or user groups.

Furthermore, certain software may have roles in addition to allowing control on each of the privileges. So, a user group may be assigned the role of analyst and also be permitted to determine dashboard refresh frequency, which is part of the administrator's privilege domain. Another situation may be that a user group is given the role of analyst but revoked the privilege of creating a category for grouping of dashboards. Such overwriting capabilities on the standard set of privileges within a role provides the leverage of using roles as a grouping of functions without limiting the capability to derive custom grouping of functions as needed within an organization.

For an effective role assignment, it is important to have a proper understanding of the organizational functions being performed by the users receiving access to the dashboards. Such information mostly resides with the department heads who are ultimately responsible for harnessing the power of dashboards within their department.

Role - Privilege Management Features	Y/N
Can a new role be created with a set of privileges as needed?	
Can the set of privileges within a role be modified?	
Can additional privileges be added to a group that is assigned a role?	
Can an existing privilege be revoked from a group that is assigned a role?	
Can a new custom privilege be added to a role?	
Can a role be assigned to a hierarchy of user groups with the ability to inherit roles?	

EXHIBIT 3.3 LIST OF FEATURES TO ASSESS ROLE PRIVILEGE MANAGEMENT CAPABILITIES

As illustrated in the previous examples, the features of the dashboard software often dictate the nuances of managing privilege domain. To evaluate any given dashboard software regarding user privilege management, the proposed list in Exhibit 3.3 may be applied. However, it is important to note that, for the most part, an inverse relationship exists between software capability and complexity. Any software allowing an extensive user privilege management may also require a well-trained administrator for that software. However, for larger deployments, this added personnel requirement is well worth it because personalized dashboards are provided to a large user base with a relatively small overhead for the software management.

CONTENT DOMAIN

The user groups are defined and the roles have been assigned, but still unanswered is the question: *What data and KPIs does a user see on a dashboard?* Answering this question leads us to the issue of *content domain*—the parameters of which would define the KPI granularity, the reports, and the alerts for each dashboard user. Managing content domain involves two aspects: (1) security and (2) relevance.

Security refers to the restriction of information delivery only to those with the privilege to access certain information. Information is inherently confidential, and every organization has its boundaries regarding who may access what information. The security framework must be created during a dashboard deployment, determining the permissions and restrictions on the content domain of each user.

Relevance refers to the filtering of the most relevant content to a given dashboard user. From all of the permitted information for a given user, an effective dashboard must present the most relevant content with flexibility for the user to access more information as needed. For example, an organization may allow all sales managers to be able to see sales numbers for all sales regions and territories. If the company has ten sales managers, one for each region, then relevance demands that each sales manager be presented with KPIs for the relevant region and the territories that fall within that region. Nevertheless, a manager may be able to retrieve any other region and territory sales if needed to compare or review adjoining regions or territories. Similarly, the manager may usually require only the latest month's KPIs along with variance compared to the previous year, but should have access to historical information and trends if needed.

A senior executive in the field of business intelligence recently pointed out the challenge of pinpointing the right content: "With the data explosion, the haystack continues to get bigger."

Managing the content domain for security and relevance requires the following levels of control:

- Dashboard level
- Report level
- Chart level
- KPI grain level
- Subject area level
- Alert level

Dashboard-level security allows withholding access to individual dashboards or a set of dashboards from any given user or user group. For example, if there are separate sets of dashboards for Sales, Customer Service, and Supply Chain, then the set of Supply Chain dashboards could be blocked off from the Sales department, and vice versa. Furthermore, a set of dashboards for senior management may consolidate high-level KPIs for all departments. Such dashboards may be secured from all other users who are not part of the senior management team.

Report-level security allows withholding access to individual reports or a set of reports from any given user or user group. It is a common practice to have embedded reports or links to reports on a given dashboard. So, if a user is not authorized to access a given report, and the report's link shows on a dashboard to which the user has access, clicking on the report link would result in a message of "access not permitted." However, it would be even more effective if the dashboard software had built-in intelligence to hide the report link from an unauthorized user. Note that best practices would dictate that the person designing a dashboard first reconcile all report links on a dashboard with the access rights for those reports and the access rights for that dashboard. In the absence of such reconciliation, the software's report-level security would be put to the test.

Chart-level security allows withholding access to individual charts from any given user or user group. Charts are visual presentations of data, and they are one of the main building blocks of dashboards. Different vendors use different terminology, such as analytic, widget, graph, and so on. Chart-level security works in a slightly different manner from report-level security in that the security is not on the chart itself but on the data being presented through the chart. So, if a chart displays data for a KPI or its grain that is not permitted to a given user, the corresponding chart will not be completely displayed and may carry an error message. If charts are parts of reports and do not represent a separate entity within the dashboard, then the report-level security as described in the previous paragraph would apply.

KPI grain-level control is key to establishing relevance. For example, in the earlier example, each of the ten sales managers were associated with their respective regional slice in a regional sales dashboard that automatically presented filtered data for the user's associated regional slice. However, each chart and report within the dashboard may also provide links to other regions and historical data, thus giving the user easy access to other authorized information. Note that KPI grain-level control may also be applied for security. For example, if the company were to block other regions' sales information to each sales manager, links to other regions would not be presented. This would make the KPI grain-level control not only related to relevance but a security feature as well.

Subject area is a surrogate layer of content grouping that helps in managing the content access to users. A subject area could be defined as a collection of dashboards, reports, charts, or KPIs. So, a user who is denied access to a given subject area will not have access to the entire collection of information grouped under that subject area. Simply put, subject area for content domain works in much the same way that user groups do to reduce repetitive tasks in that they allow the management of *collections* rather than of *individuals*. For example, a subject area of Finance may be restricted to senior management and the accounting department. So, all of the dashboards, charts, and reports falling within the Finance subject area will be invisible to the rest of dashboard users. Note that all dashboard vendors may not have a subject area concept or may refer to this layer with a different term. Also, some software packages may have subject area controls limited to a collection of dashboards or KPIs, which may not encompass all of the dashboard elements.

Alert-level control is another feature used to establish relevance within the content domain. Alerts help manage exceptions and alert the user of any unusual change or threshold value reached for any KPI. So, the action resulting from alerts needs to be assigned to those users who need to be informed of the exceptions. Continuing the earlier example of ten sales managers for the ten regions, each regional alert needs to generate e-mails and on-screen warning messages for the sales managers of the corresponding region. Similarly, the territorial alerts need to be assigned to the corresponding territory reps and the associated sales manager responsible for that territory. Although there may be no security reason for restricting one sales manager from knowing any other region's alerts, this information would simply not be relevant. (An in-depth discussion on the topic of dashboard alerts follows in Chapter 5.)

The security and relevance controls together contribute to the delivery of personalized dashboard content. Therefore, it is imperative to understand the entire user base and establish a structured framework for personalized dashboard deployment.

ENDNOTE

1. Bernard Liautaud, Chairman and CEO, Business Objects, *Business Objects Americas Partner Summit keynote speech*, Palm Springs, California, May 18, 2004.

4

PRESENTATION

Design, Layout, and Navigation

Popular Internet travel sites, auction portals, and search engines have set the standards—we all have learned on our own to gainfully use them. Enterprise dashboards must be just as intuitive.

This chapter addresses the third aspect of the dashboarding process: *How to present information?*

Creating the meta-information and audience frameworks in the dashboarding process is much like building the foundation and structure of a house. After those steps, you are ready to create the interior and exterior design of the structure, replete with doors, windows, passages, painting, and the final touches. The dashboard presentation work may be broken down into three areas: (1) design, (2) layout, and (3) navigation.

DASHBOARD DESIGN

A well-designed dashboard must have an aesthetic appeal and deploy powerful visualization to convey a wealth of information within a limited space. Some of the key elements important to dashboard design are the following:

- Screen graphics and colors
- Selection of appropriate chart types

- Animation with relevance
- Optimal content placement

Screen Graphics and Colors

Screen graphics and colors are important in building the visual framework of the dashboard. Unlike reports, users expect much greater visual appeal from dashboards. Often, dashboards display a company banner with colors that are consistent with the company's logo or brand colors. Preference should be given to light and neutral colors for banners, navigation tabs, and borders within a dashboard. The color palette should not interfere with or distract from the key messages and information displayed on the dashboard. Light blue, light gray, or light beige are good choices. Charts and other key message delivery systems should have their own color scheme to differentiate them from background, aesthetic, or functional elements.

For the same reasons, extraneous graphics such as company logos or project logos must not be given too much prominence in a business dashboard. Such graphics are important to reinforce a company's branding, but they must be used with discretion because a dashboard screen's real estate is expensive.

Certain dashboard software may allow each user to change the dashboard colors to suit his or her taste. After all, color is a matter of individual taste. Nevertheless, most users will be satisfied with the default colors set by the administrator. Therefore, it is advised to use neutral colors that appeal to the largest segment of the population.

Colors may also play the role of content separators. For example, a company may use different background colors for various department dashboards. Other types of colored content differentiation may involve the basic dimensions of geography, product, and time. For example, each region or product group may be associated with a certain background color or tabs color. Such color protocols ensure presentation consistency and faster assimilation of information.

Chart Types

After resolving the base colors and graphics, the next area of design focus would be chart selections for presenting the key performance indicators (KPIs) and the underlying data. Selection of appropriate charts requires a good blend of analytical thinking and artistic rendering. Depending on the information being presented, certain chart types are most appropriate. For example, if relative shares need to be displayed, a pie chart is invariably the perfect fit. If a trend needs to be shown, a line chart works well. If two metrics need to be compared, a dual column or bar chart is a good rule of thumb.

However, in many instances the choice of charts may not be so obvious, requiring a degree of flexibility and creativity. Some of the contemporary, popular chart types include traffic lights, speedometers or dials, thermometers, donuts, and bubble charts. The choice of charts also depends on area constraints on the dashboard. For example, if the available area is narrow but high, a thermometer representation may work well instead of a speedometer, which requires more of a square-shaped area. Similarly, traffic lights may represent KPIs effectively within a relatively small area—just enough to have three small circles representing the three colored lamps in a traffic light. This model is also effective in conveying the relative performance of the charted KPIs: a red light jumps out at the viewer, drawing immediate attention.

Charts also demand internal color choices: the colors of the pies, bars, speedometer thresholds, and so on. The default colors supplied by any standard dashboard software are often well selected with a professional designer's input. However, a dashboard creator may have the liberty to change these colors at his or her discretion. If a dashboard is being deployed for a large audience, it is a good practice to seek advice from a professional designer in selecting the chart colors, so that they may have a positive visual appeal to the largest possible number of users. As every professional designer knows, there is a lot of science in color choice and its relative placements. Even more important, a spectrum of emotional messages is associated with each color.

Animation with Relevance

Animation with relevance is a powerful feature that conveys valuable information to the viewer. This feature uses advanced visual capabilities (if provided by the software) to meaningfully interact with users. For example, if a user has the mouse hovering over a certain slice on a pie chart, corresponding metrics within other charts on that dashboard related to that slice would automatically highlight. In another instance, a speedometer displaying metrics relevant to that pie will have its needle swing to the appropriate value through real-time animation. Exhibits 4.1 and 4.2 demonstrate these features on a dashboard.

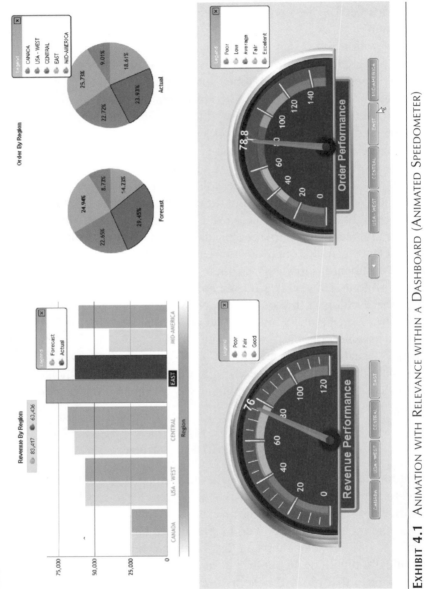

EXHIBIT 4.1 ANIMATION WITH RELEVANCE WITHIN A DASHBOARD (ANIMATED SPEEDOMETER)

Courtesy: iDashboards

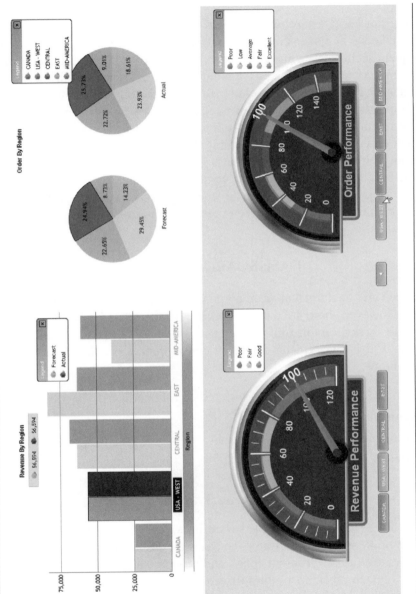

Exhibit 4.2 Animation with Relevance within a Dashboard (Relevant Highlighting)

Courtesy: iDashboards

Optimal Content Placement

Last, but not least, regarding dashboard design considerations is the aspect of optimal content placement and layout. (Layout is discussed in detail in the subsequent section.) The most important principle of dashboard layout is that of limiting content. Overloading a single dashboard screen with too much content may create a sense of clutter that would overwhelm the user. The most important KPIs for each user would rarely lead to an overload, but it may be tempting to create an information overload if the designer has not done enough due diligence to determine the top-priority KPIs for each user. Invariably, any good dashboard software would also allow business users to perform limited customization that would enable them to choose the KPIs that are most important for them to track, and they want those KPIs displayed on the first dashboard screen presented after login.

DASHBOARD LAYOUT

It may be valid to claim that dashboard layout is an element of the dashboard design. However, there are enough specific details related to layout to warrant a full section on this topic.

Some of the key elements requiring consideration in a dashboard layout are as follows:

- Number of windows/frames within the dashboard
- Symmetry and proportions
- Computer resolution considerations
- Context selection

Windows/Frames

Most of the leading dashboard software packages provide the flexibility to create multiple windows (or frames) on a single dashboard screen. This facilitates the insertion of different charts and reports within each window, independent of each other. Also, the software may allow independent control of the sizing of each window by simple drag-and-drop editing.

It is prudent not to overwhelm the dashboard viewer with a large number of such windows, because each window places a demand on user attention. The overall screen must not create a sense of information overload for the user that may eventually lead to oversight. Therefore, it is a good practice to have no more than six windows on a dashboard screen. Four windows are optimal, but if absolutely necessary, six windows may still serve as an effective display. However, exceeding the six-window limit is not recommended.

Note that most software would allow making these windows seamless by removing the visible partitions among them and making the different displays appear as a single integrated page view.

Symmetry and Proportions

Symmetry and proportions of the windows are also important to maintain an effective visual presentation. Most likely, the dashboard creation team consists of analysts, subject matter experts from the business domain, and software experts from the IT domain. Unfortunately, none of these people have the requisite training or experience in professional design. This may often lead to creation of asymmetric and out-of-proportion window layouts, as developers, who are inexperienced with issues of design, take full liberty with the dashboard software's capability to size and shape the windows.

It is a good rule of thumb to have uniformly sized windows. Irregularly sized windows may lead to unintended highlighting and diminishing of the importance of displayed information. Exhibit 4.3 presents some possible window configurations for a typical dashboard layout.

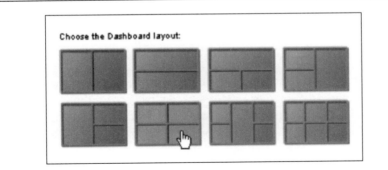

EXHIBIT 4.3 STANDARDIZED WINDOW LAYOUTS FOR A DASHBOARD

Computer Resolution

Computer screen resolution is an important consideration for deciding the window placements within a dashboard. Currently, it is best practice to design dashboards optimally for a 1024 × 768 screen resolution. This eliminates the need for horizontal scrolling associated with higher resolutions such as 1152 × 864, 1280 × 1024, or beyond. Users with 800 × 600 resolution may have to scroll to view the full dashboard's content. However, most likely this would affect no more than 20% of the user base, although this number requires evaluation for the specific install base for the dashboard. With an increase in the quality and size of desktop monitors and laptop screens, an overwhelming majority of business users have a setting of 1024 × 768 or higher that leverages the larger viewing areas of their screen.

Best efforts must be made to design the dashboard such that a 1024 × 768 screen resolution requires no horizontal or vertical scrolling to view the complete dashboard. Dashboards exceeding 720 pixels in height may be deployed if the lower portion of the dashboard is used to merely provide links to relevant reports and charts. However, important KPIs requiring regular user attention must never be placed outside of the viewing area that requires scrolling to be viewed.

Context Selection

Context selection refers to the placement of content among the various windows within the dashboard. Typically, the subject matter experts within each business division for which dashboards are being deployed make such determinations. If the dashboard creators belong to the IT or analytical domains, they are strongly advised to consult the designated subject matter experts within each of the divisions. Dashboards must provide a view into the business, and only the business users know best how they view and interrelate various charts and reports to extract critical business information.

To ensure a positive reception of a dashboard deployment by end users, it is a good practice to elicit early input and feedback from the user base. Context selection and navigation are the two most important areas requiring end-user input (see Exhibit 4.4 for a proposed dashboard layout for an iron-ore mining company). Other elements of dashboard design and layout may be left to the best practices and input from professional designers and business analysts.

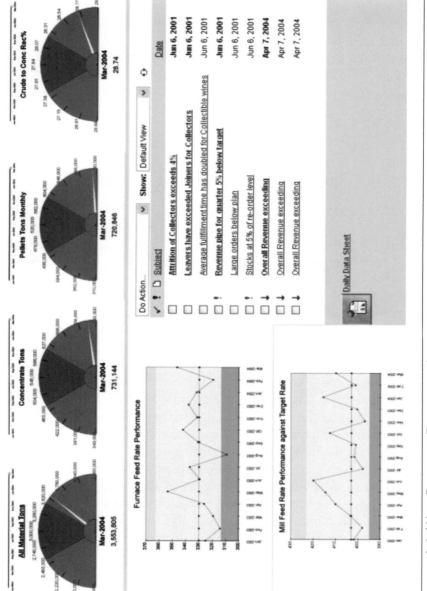

EXHIBIT 4.4 WELL-BALANCED DASHBOARD LAYOUT

DASHBOARD NAVIGATION

Navigation involves determining how the total information will be divided across different dashboard screens as well as linking charts and reports to allow user drill-down for greater details.

Some of the key elements requiring consideration for dashboard navigation are the following:

- Information grouping and hierarchy
- Tabs and pivots
- Context drill-down

Information Grouping and Hierarchy

Information grouping and hierarchy refers to the creation of dashboard groupings according to the information presented in them. Such groupings and hierarchies also help determine which group of dashboards falls at what node of the information hierarchy, given the importance and priority of the information content.

Different dashboard software packages may allow different levels within the dashboard hierarchy. However, two levels of hierarchy are fairly standard across all of the leading software. Each of the dashboards in the first level would have tabs or links to a set of children dashboards (second-level dashboards). So, the user community must determine how to group the information and how the dashboard grouping and hierarchy is created in accordance. For example, Sales may want to see the first level of dashboards as each product line aggregated across all regions and the second level as each of the regions within the product line. Another scenario could be just the reverse—the first level of dashboards as each region aggregated across all product lines and the second level as each of the product lines within the region. Another example would find a dashboard hierarchy to view Web metrics displaying total Web hits for the entire Web site on the first level and Web metrics for each of the product lines on the second level. Exhibit 4.5 demonstrates a typical dashboard grouping and hierarchy.

Tabs and Pivots

Tabs and pivots help design the user experience in navigating across the dashboard groups. Often, the dashboard software limits which of these two features may be used, unless custom programming is done.

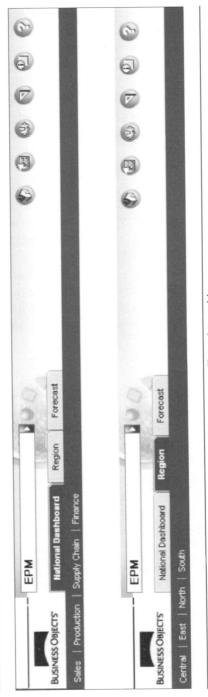

EXHIBIT 4.5 EXAMPLE OF A DASHBOARD GROUPING WITH A TWO-LEVEL HIERARCHY

Courtesy: Business Objects

Tabs are links presented horizontally or vertically with a brief title on which the user may click to see the corresponding dashboard. This is a very popular format found on most Web sites to segment information. Pivots are drop-down lists that allow users to select any one of the listed dashboards to view. If there are many dashboards, pivots offer an advantage because tabs are subject to the limitation of screen width. If there are fewer dashboards, tabs are preferable because the tab titles are easily evident to the user. There is no need to click on a drop-down menu to see the list.

Context Drill-Down

Context drill-down is an extremely important aspect of the user navigation experience. Drill-down features provide additional details when a user clicks on a specific chart or report. Context drill-down is essentially a link with the added intelligence of knowing which data point on a chart was clicked on. A drill-down has two components: (1) source and (2) destination.

Source requires capturing the chart or report that has been clicked on along with the specific data point value that the user had mouse-over for the click. The data point context is then passed on to the destination, which must have a smart filtering capability to present the information relevant to the data point that was clicked on. The source chart information is subsequently used for the user to navigate back to the point of origin.

Destination chart accepts the source data point parameter and presents the filtered chart or report. For example, if the user clicks on a U.S. map with mouse-over on the state of California, the destination chart or report will present information relevant to California only. The power of this feature is that the user is immediately directed to the relevant section (dealing with California) of the report as compared to scrolling through a long report with 50 states. Similarly, it requires only one link on the source map that automatically passes the state as the parameter.

A note of caution: Some dashboard software may not provide context linking capability, which means the destination chart is presented without filtering the data per the context. This presents a major limitation in designing effective navigation and a good dashboarding experience. An absence of context linking will prevent the destination report from being filtered for the specific point of interest being drilled down.

It is important to determine the drill-down path in terms of source-destination pairing. As emphasized in the earlier section, it is a good practice to receive early input and feedback from the user base to determine optimal drill-down paths. For example, if a sales manager clicks on a chart showing regional sales trend by month, should the destination chart present the sales trend for children territories or should it have the sales by product line for the month clicked on? Or should the drill-down lead to another dashboard with both these details for the region? In some cases, software may allow more than one link to be clicked on within a chart. However, the concept of drill-down context can work with a single destination only. A detailed discussion of the resolution of these navigation issues for an effective dashboard deployment takes place in Chapter 6 on Storyboarding.

5

Dashboard Alerts

What are your red flag mechanisms? We found no evidence that the good-to-great companies had more or better information than the comparison companies. None. Both sets of companies had virtually identical access to good information. The key, then, lies not in better information, but in turning information into information that cannot be ignored.

—Jim Collins[1]

Jim Collins, best-selling author and management researcher, emphasizes the importance of building red flag mechanisms for urgent delivery of information requiring immediate attention. Dashboards facilitate the building of such mechanisms through alerts (also referred to as alarms).

Alerts are integral to the dashboard concept in that they transform the dashboard from a graphical information presentation into a live console for managing organizational processes and performance. Effective dashboard deployment must facilitate easy management of alerts. This management process involves three components: (1) rules, (2) actions, and (3) recipients (see Exhibit 5.1).

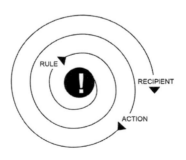

Exhibit 5.1 Sequential Components within a Dashboard Alert System

RULES

The rules component (also referred to as rules engine) helps in managing the business rules at work behind the creation of alerts. The dashboard drives the alerts by monitoring the rules. Following is an example of how rules work to create user alerts.

A user alert must be created if the data indicates:

- One point outside a prespecified limit
- X points in a row increasing (or decreasing)
- X points in a row on the same side of the reference value
- X points in a row alternating up and down

Note, the value of X may be specified on a case-by-case basis for each rule.

Obviously, each organization will have its own sets of rules for different areas of business. The effectiveness of a rules engine in a dashboard is determined by how much flexibility it has to accommodate any possible business rule required for driving alerts. Moreover, the configuration of such business rules should be possible through a user-friendly graphical interface that does not require any software programming skills (see Exhibit 5.2).

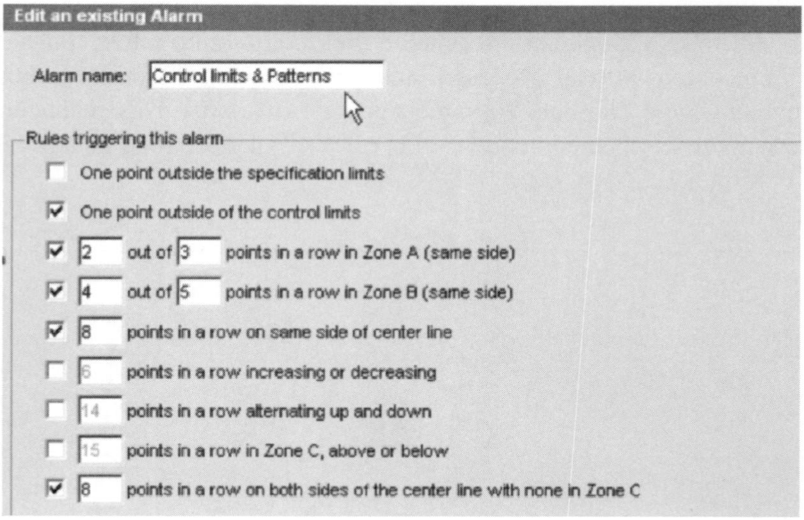

EXHIBIT 5.2 ALARM TEMPLATE FOR STATISTICAL PROCESS CONTROL
Courtesy: Business Objects

As mentioned earlier, the dashboarding software must balance the need for flexibility with an awareness of the consequences of increased complexity. Building in a great amount of flexibility in the form of many options and features requires users to have an in-depth understanding of the software's capability and functioning. Thus, a higher level of user training is required to understand and leverage all of the software functions and features to optimally use the available flexibility. The area of the rules engine for managing alerts is perhaps the area most affected by this dilemma that I refer to as the *comflex syndrome*.

The *comflex syndrome* relates to the rules engine in the following way: If the system is flexible, but complex to configure, then it inhibits the business users' ability to define their rules and customize the alerts system to most effectively manage their specific aspect of the business. This, in turn, means that business users depend on those very few people within the organization who are trained to leverage the rules engine. This immediately limits the power of dashboards to be fully leveraged as a live control interface to monitor processes and business domain at various levels within the organization.

A rules engine can be powerful if it fulfills three key requirements:

1. Ability to create a complex rule that is a logical combination of multiple individual rules
2. Ability to monitor the rules
3. Ability to launch actions that may manage process flow within the organization

Complex rule creation helps in grouping the rules such that if any of them is triggered, the same action is instantiated by the dashboard software. Another application of complex rules would be to create a logical condition requiring the software to check against multiple rules at once. This "checking" capability helps create a sophisticated early warning system (EWS) to capture shifts in business that may be inherently complex and require a combination of different measures.

For example, a simple rule in which an alert is created when sales are down compared to a previous month is easy to create. However, if a complex rule could have detected a sales-lowering trend during the middle of the month, maybe a month-end promotion could have been planned to help increase sales. A complex rule in such a situation could be a combination of average daily sales comparison against previous month, week-to-week sales comparison, and a two-week moving average trend. When a certain threshold is reached in these three individual rules, an alert is issued as follows:

- *Daily sales monitoring.* Average daily sales against previous month (five or more days lower)
- *Weekly sales comparison.* Consecutive week sales comparison (two consecutive weeks lower)
- *Two-week sales trend.* Two-week moving average of sales (10% below previous month's weekly average)

  Alert: When any two of these three rules trigger alerts, send a "Lower Sales Trend" alert.

As evident from this example, dashboard alerts are best leveraged when the rules engine can model complex situations, indicating an early warning and providing opportunities to act before it is too late. The creative power of harnessing a rules engine is only limited by an individual's ability to model the business factors and processes.

Authoring powerful and effective rules to model business processes is best achieved with a group effort involving business domain experts and analysts who can model those processes through metrics. Business domain experts who typically may not have formal training or experience in analysis may often have missed opportunities to create powerful early warning systems. The process of creating an effective EWS is an evolving one. As more patterns are determined through an ongoing analysis of cause-and-effect factors within the business environment, which itself is in a constant state of evolution, the system can be modified and improved. Exhibit 5.3 illustrates a complex rule creation interface.

The second key characteristic of the rules engine is *monitoring*. In other words, when and with what frequency would the dashboard software execute the checks against the rules? Monitoring includes scheduling features such as time/day selection, periodicity, and external triggers to invoke the rules engine.

The following are some examples of monitoring options that may be required during an alert configuration:

- hh:mm daily
- hh:mm specific day of the week
- hh:mm specific day of the month
- hh:mm specific dates of the month
- hh:mm on intervals of X days
- Round-the-clock at intervals of X minutes

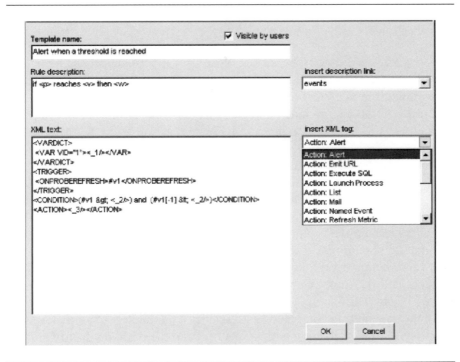

EXHIBIT 5.3 RULE CONFIGURATION TEMPLATE WITH DIFFERENT ALERT ACTIONS
Courtesy: Business Objects

- Triggered by a software command, which in turn can be an action for another alert

ACTIONS

The second characteristic of a powerful alert system—actions—will also have a direct influence on the process flow. As implied by the term, this part of the alert system helps define the follow-up action when an alert occurs. Most commonly, the actions would constitute sending an e-mail to the relevant people authorized and responsible for the specific area of information.

Dashboard software must facilitate the definition of the e-mail content as part of the action. Typical content features of the e-mail could be:

- Title and brief description
- Link to a dashboard showing the relevant reports and charts
- Attached or embedded report(s) within the e-mail

The alert creation interface must allow a user to pick one or more of these features to define the e-mail content. Often, a self-guiding wizard that prompts the user step-by-step for each of the content elements is helpful in configuring an alert. The other aspect of the wizard must be to select the recipients for the e-mail. This ties back into the security framework and is discussed in greater detail in the next section.

E-mail action is sufficient when the reaction to an alert invariably requires human decision or the lack of an immediate inaction is not adverse. When either of these factors is not the case, a system action must be created. For example, in the case of fraud detection, the cost of inaction may be too adverse to wait for a human intervention after an alert is created. An immediate action to suspend the alerted account would be needed. Many other instances might warrant system actions as well (e.g., optimal inventory levels, supply chain management, order management, national security, financial market conditions).

System action works best when the parameters for the action are well defined, and the trade-off between the risks of such an action being wrong versus inaction is heavily weighted against inaction. System action mostly involves transmitting commands with specified parameters to a software system. Facilitating such communications between the dashboard software and another system may involve integration work. Typical system actions may have one or more of the following elements:

- Data updates in a database
- Software process launch
- Software process halt
- Change of specification limits in quality control charts
- Change of specification limits in process controls
- Change of parameters for a forecasting and/or production planning system
- Sending audio or visual signals
- Creating text messages for phones or PDAs
- Sending pager signals or prerecorded phone calls

However, as best practices indicate, all system actions must be recorded (logged) within the dashboard software, and the corresponding alert for each action must be available for human scrutiny. A system action should always be accompanied by an e-mail to the appropriate personnel to inform them of the action.

As evident from the types of actions listed, these require prior integration work to make such communications happen seamlessly with limited controlling power assigned to the dashboard. A sophisticated alert-action system could potentially make a dashboard the central console for business activity monitoring (BAM), quality control, enterprise performance management (EPM), financial trading, and the list goes on and extends into the future.

RECIPIENTS

Having determined the rule and action(s), the third and last step in creation of an alert is determining the recipient(s). The alert configuration tool within the dashboard must allow an easy selection of alert recipients. The selection interface must facilitate inclusion of individuals and user groups defined within the dashboard framework.

For example, if an alert is defined to appear in the event that Region 1 sales drop below 10% of the monthly target for the region, then the alert may be configured to initiate an action, an e-mail to the Region 1 user group, as well as the VP of Sales. In other words, all users defined within the Region 1 user group would receive the alert.

Effective recipient selection interface facilitates user search and easy navigation of the users' list when the dashboard deployment is across a large user base. It also allows the selection of several user groups across different hierarchies as recipients of an alert action.

Depending on the scope of recipients, alerts may be divided into two categories: (1) personal and (2) public alerts.

Personal Alerts

Any dashboard user, to help monitor key performance indicators specific to an individual domain of responsibility, may create personal alerts. The actions of such an alert are limited, and the recipient of such action would be that specific individual only.

Public Alerts

The ability to create public alerts may be confined to a restricted user base who may select any number of users and user groups to receive a given alert. Public alerts may be a privilege that is assigned to certain individuals or roles, as described in Chapter 3. Besides making the recipient selection unrestricted, public alerts may also allow a full spectrum of actions, such as system actions that may otherwise be restricted from personal alerts.

USER HANDLING

Once an alert has reached its rightful destination, the dashboard must allow users to archive or discard the alerts. Much like e-mail software, an effective user-handling interface must also allow for organizing alerts into different folders as well as assigning alerts into different categories.

The following are some of the alert types provided within a dashboard alert system:

- Critical Alert
- Important Alert
- Informational Alert
- Public Alert
- Private Alert
- Unread Alert

In Exhibit 5.4, highlighted alerts (in bold text) indicate that they have not been clicked on. The different signs on the left margin of the alerts indicate the type of alert.

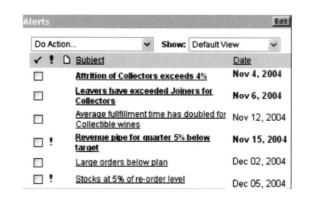

EXHIBIT 5.4 AN ALERT INTERFACE

Effective alert handling must also include the capability to forward alerts to other dashboard users. This facilitates effective communication to address a situation that may require the attention of several people within the organization.

COLLABORATION

Alerts must also link to a collaboration system that allows all those receiving the alerts to participate in a relevant discussion regarding each alert. An effective collaboration system contains all the critical features of a discussion forum. Although great detail on this topic would be beyond the scope of this book, some of the critical features of a discussion forum linked to an alert would be the following:

- Ability for each participant to easily notice if there is a new posting
- Ability to track and display the individual's identity corresponding to each posting
- Ability to select an option for receiving e-mail for each new posting
- Ability to attach a document(s) to each posting
- Ability to edit a posting by the individual who created the posting while restricting others from modifying it
- Ability to track the time stamp and sequence of postings while displaying as a sequential thread (in descending order of the posted sequence)
- Ability to search for a specific word or phrase through the postings

ENDNOTE

1. Jim Collins, *Good to Great: Why Some Companies Make the Leap ... and Others Don't* (New York: HarperBusiness, 2001).

6

STORYBOARDING

A picture is better than a thousand words. A sequence of pictures presenting a live scenario on a dashboard is even far better.

The term *storyboarding* is derived from the field of multimedia design in which animation is first conceptualized through a panel of sketches outlining the scene sequence and major changes of action. In other words, storyboarding is the process of telling a story for animation through static images. Similar to a multimedia concept that may involve defining user interaction and corresponding response, a good dashboard is replete with user interactions and dashboard responses to those actions.

Storyboarding brings together all key areas of the dashboarding process that have been discussed so far: meta-information, audience, presentation, and alerts. The following steps may be followed through a dashboard storyboarding exercise:

1. Identify key user groupings
2. Identify key dashboard groupings
3. Determine the privilege matrix: user groups and dashboard groups
4. Sketch a dashboard layout for each dashboard group
5. Sketch a navigation sequence for each dashboard component on every dashboard template

Note that storyboarding is a high-level exercise that does not delve into the nitty-gritty of how and where to get the information. During this step, it is simply assumed that any information required for the dashboard display can be retrieved from the information biosphere of the organization (see Exhibit 2.2).

Storyboarding is a group exercise and is the culmination of the requirements gathering phase for a dashboard deployment. A qualified team for storyboarding would include business user representatives from each user group, a business analyst(s), a dashboard software expert, and preferably a business intelligence (BI) expert who is knowledgeable about the organization's existing BI infrastructure. Storyboarding may be done using any one or more of the familiar tools such as a word processor, spreadsheet program, drawing software, presentation software, or an image editor. Almost any software that helps put a sketch together would be appropriate.

SCENARIO 1

This storyboarding scenario deals with a dashboard deployment for the sales group of a large computer manufacturer with a worldwide presence divided into three markets: (1) the Americas, (2) Asia Pacific, and (3) Europe and the Middle East. The company's business and administration is divided into two groups as follows:

1. Computers: Computers, Desktops, Notebooks, Servers, Handhelds, Monitors, Projectors
2. Peripherals: Printers, Multifunctions, Copiers, Scanners, Fax, Storage, Supplies and Accessories

For this scenario, we will follow the five-step storyboarding process as follows:

Step 1: The different user groups are determined with their high-level information needs. The user groups and their relative hierarchy are shown in Exhibit 6.1. *Note:* Only one region and one territory have been expanded to the full hierarchy. Similar hierarchies are prevalent within other markets of Europe, Middle East, and Asia Pacific.

Step 2: The dashboard groups are determined. The dashboard groups and their hierarchy are shown in Exhibit 6.2, which shows a three-level dashboard hierarchy with dashboard groupings per geographic sales regions and the business group. Note that each node shown in the exhibit represents a dashboard with metrics, key per-

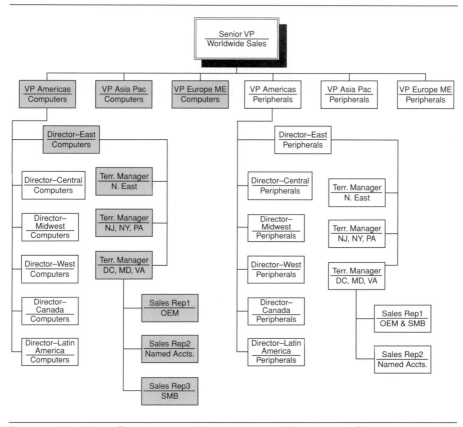

EXHIBIT 6.1 USER GROUPS AND HIERARCHY FOR WORLDWIDE SALES ORGANIZATION

formance indicators (KPIs), and alerts for the corresponding region and the business group.

Step 3: The user group and dashboard group privilege matrix is determined. Exhibit 6.3 shows this matrix.

Note that users at vice president levels may access dashboards for their own markets as well as other markets, regions, and business groups that do not fall under their domain of responsibility. Users at the director level can access only the regions within their domain of responsibility, but for that region they may access the dashboard for the counterpart business group

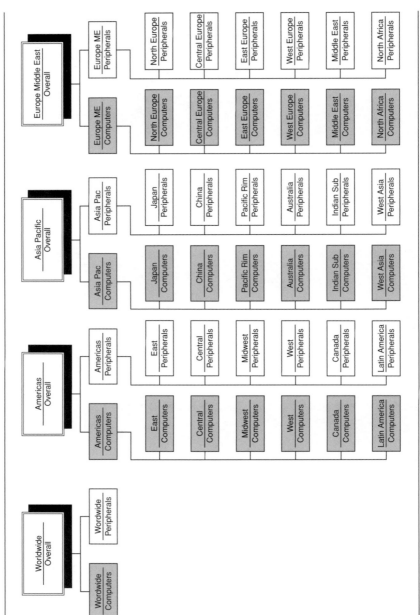

EXHIBIT 6.2 DASHBOARD GROUPS AND HIERARCHY FOR WORLDWIDE SALES ORGANIZATION

Dashboard Groups	Senior VP	Computers			Peripherals		
		Market VP	Region Director	Terr. Manager	Market VP	Region Director	Terr. Manager
Computers							
Worldwide	Δ						
Americas	Δ	Δ			Δ		
Asia Pacific	Δ	Δ			Δ		
Europe ME	Δ	Δ			Δ		
Regions	Δ	Δ	D		Δ	D	
Territories			D	D		D	
Peripherals							
Worldwide	Δ						
Americas	Δ	Δ			Δ		
Asia Pacific	Δ	Δ			Δ		
Europe ME	Δ	Δ			Δ		
Regions	Δ	Δ	D		Δ	D	
Territories			D			D	D

D denotes access only to those dashboards for the specific region or territory, which are within the domain of the user's responsibility.
Δ denotes the user has access to all dashboards within the corresponding dashboard group.

EXHIBIT 6.3 PRIVILEGE MATRIX FOR USER GROUPS: DASHBOARD GROUPS

(computers or peripherals). However, users at the manager level are restricted to the territory and business group for which they are directly responsible.

Step 4: Sketch a dashboard layout for each of the cross-sections of dashboard and user group nodes. Exhibits 6.4 and 6.5 show sample dashboard layouts for markets and regions for the computers and peripheral groups. Similar dashboard layouts may be made for other node intersections.

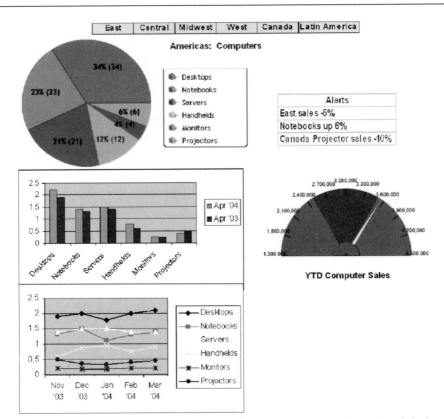

Note: The tabs on the top of the dashboard indicate navigation to the regional dashboards within Americas.

EXHIBIT 6.4 DASHBOARD SKETCH FOR THE MARKET OF AMERICAS—COMPUTERS

Step 5: Sketch the navigation paths if the user were to click on any part of a dashboard. Exhibits 6.6 and 6.7 show the drill-down scenario for the regional computer group dashboard. Similar navigational sequence sketches may be done for the peripherals group and for other geographic nodes.

Note that the purpose of charts in a storyboarding template is to simply demonstrate the dashboard layouts and user navigation experience. The storyboard templates (Exhibits 6.4 through 6.7) were built using chart images, spreadsheets, and presentation software.

The illustrations in Exhibits 6.4 through 6.7 show the storyboarding process to successfully begin dashboard deployment for this scenario. Building a comprehensive storyboard would involve business stakeholders, subject matter experts, analysts, dashboard software experts, and IT support. Such a group effort helps clarify the business rules and information needs and builds a consensus, all of which are critical for successful dashboard deployment.

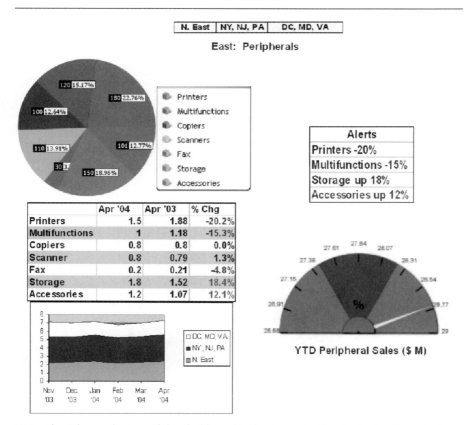

Note: The tabs on the top of the dashboard indicate navigation to the territory dashboards within the East region.

EXHIBIT 6.5 DASHBOARD SKETCH FOR THE EAST REGION—PERIPHERALS

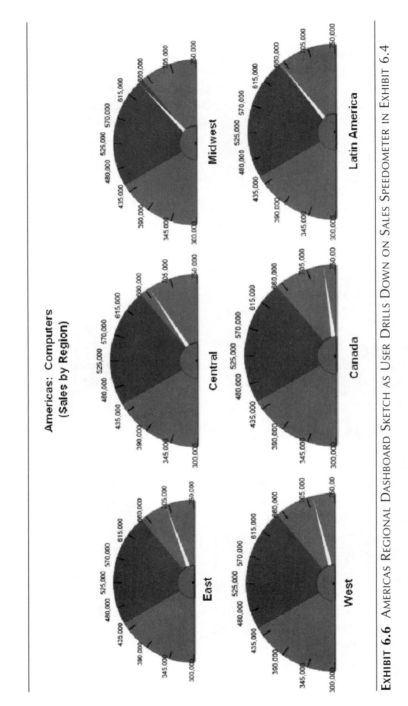

EXHIBIT 6.6 AMERICAS REGIONAL DASHBOARD SKETCH AS USER DRILLS DOWN ON SALES SPEEDOMETER IN EXHIBIT 6.4

Eastern Region: Computers

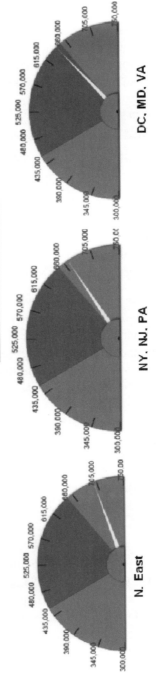

	YTD
Desktops	250,000
Notebooks	180,000
Servers	109,000
Handhelds	72,000
Monitors	49,000
Projectors	42,000
Total Computers	702,000

Legend: —♦— Desktops —■— Notebooks Servers Handhelds —✳— Monitors —●— Projectors

Chart axis: 2.5, 2, 1.5, 1, 0.5, 0

Time axis: Nov '03, Dec '03, Jan '04, Feb '04, Mar '04

N. East NY. NJ. PA DC. MD. VA

EXHIBIT 6.7 EASTERN REGION DASHBOARD SKETCH AS USER DRILLS DOWN ON THE EAST SPEEDOMETER IN EXHIBIT 6.6

SCENARIO 2

This storyboarding scenario deals with a dashboard deployment for the North American Customer Service division of a large software company. The company's customer service administration is divided into three groups and respective subgroups across three regions as follows:

1. Server Applications: CRM, ERP
2. Hosted Applications: CRM, ERP
3. Developer Tools: Windows, Unix, Mobile

North American Regions—East, Central, West

Step 1: The different user groups are determined with their high-level information needs. The user groups and their relative hierarchy are shown in Exhibit 6.8.

Each group of Customer Service (CS) Engineers has several software engineers with expertise in their specific areas of software and serving their respective territories (i.e., East, Central, West). The territories are determined per time zone, and the CS engineers maintain their work hours accordingly. Customer service calls are automatically routed to the appropriate group per the time zone of the caller.

Step 2: The dashboard groups are determined. The dashboard groups and their hierarchy are shown in Exhibit 6.9, which shows a three-level dashboard hierarchy with dashboard groupings per the customer service regions and the software group. Note that each node shown in the exhibit represents a dashboard with metrics, KPIs, and alerts for the corresponding region and the software group or subgroup.

Step 3: User group and dashboard group privilege matrix is determined. Exhibit 6.10 shows this matrix.

Step 4: Dashboard layout is sketched for each of the cross-sections of dashboard and user group nodes. Exhibit 6.11 shows a sample dashboard layout for the Eastern region for the Hosted CRM software group. Similar dashboard layouts may be made for other nodes of the intersection matrix.

(text continues on page 83)

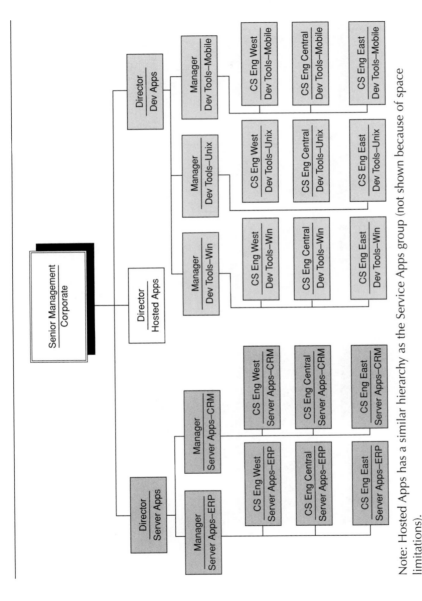

Note: Hosted Apps has a similar hierarchy as the Service Apps group (not shown because of space limitations).

EXHIBIT 6.8 USER GROUPS AND THEIR HIERARCHY FOR NORTH AMERICAN CUSTOMER SERVICE (CS) DIVISION

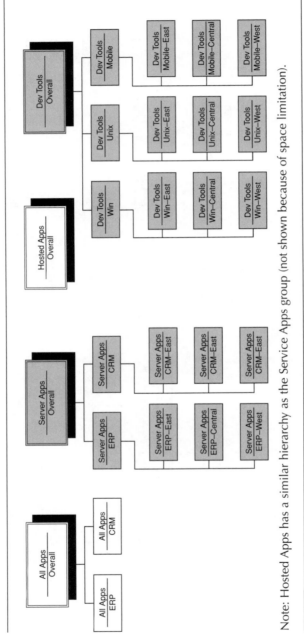

Note: Hosted Apps has a similar hierarchy as the Service Apps group (not shown because of space limitation).

EXHIBIT 6.9 DASHBOARD GROUPS AND HIERARCHY FOR NORTH AMERICAN CUSTOMER SERVICE (CS) DIVISION

Dashboard Groups	Senior Management	Server Apps				Hosted Apps				Dev Tools				
		Director	Manager–ERP	Manager–CRM	CS Engineer	Director	Manager–ERP	Manager–CRM	CS Engineer	Director	Manager–Win	Manager–Unix	Manager–Mobile	CS Engineer
All Apps	Δ													
ERP N. America	Δ													
CRM N. America	Δ													
Dev Tools N. America	Δ													
Server Apps														
ERP N. America	Δ	Δ												
CRM N. America	Δ	Δ												
ERP Regions	Δ	Δ	Δ		D									
CRM Regions	Δ	Δ		Δ	D									
Hosted Apps														
ERP N. America	Δ	Δ				Δ								
CRM N. America	Δ	Δ				Δ								
ERP Regions	Δ	Δ				Δ	Δ		D					
CRM Regions	Δ	Δ				Δ		Δ	D					
Dev Tools														
Win N. America	Δ	Δ								Δ				
Unix N. America	Δ	Δ								Δ				
Mobile N. America	Δ	Δ								Δ				
Win Regions	Δ	Δ								Δ	Δ			D
Unix Regions	Δ	Δ								Δ		Δ		D
Mobile Regions	Δ	Δ								Δ			Δ	D

D denotes that the user has access to the dashboard for the specific software group and region for which the user is directly responsible.

Δ denotes that the user has access to all dashboards in the corresponding software group.

EXHIBIT 6.10 PRIVILEGE MATRIX FOR USER GROUPS: DASHBOARD GROUPS

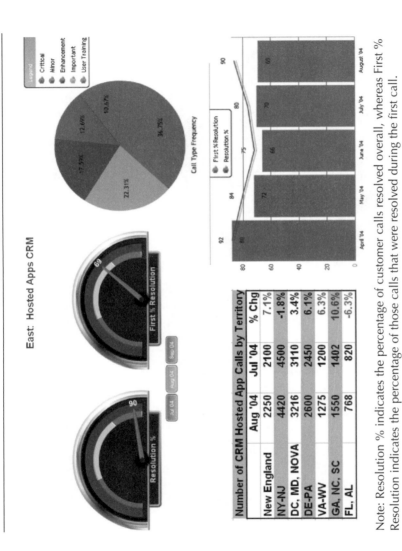

East: Hosted Apps CRM

Number of CRM Hosted App Calls by Territory			
	Aug '04	Jul '04	% Chg
New England	2250	2100	7.1%
NY-NJ	4420	4500	-1.8%
DC, MD, NOVA	3216	3110	3.4%
DE-PA	2600	2450	6.1%
VA-WV	1275	1200	6.3%
GA, NC, SC	1550	1402	10.6%
FL, AL	768	820	-6.3%

Note: Resolution % indicates the percentage of customer calls resolved overall, whereas First % Resolution indicates the percentage of those calls that were resolved during the first call.

Exhibit 6.11 Dashboard Layout Sketch for Eastern Region for the Hosted Apps CRM Group

Step 5: Sketch the navigation paths if the user were to click on any part of a dashboard. Exhibits 6.12 and 6.13 show the drill-down scenario for the Eastern CRM group dashboard. Similar navigational sequence sketches may be done for the other software groups and for other geographic nodes.

The illustrations in Exhibits 6.8 through 6.13 show the storyboarding process to successfully begin dashboard deployment for this scenario.

Note that users at the senior management level may access over all North America as well as the three regions for all software groups. Users at the director level can access all regions for the software group within their domain of responsibility as well as for their counterparts, but they cannot access the total across all three software groups (All Applications). Users at the manager level are restricted to the software group for which they are directly responsible

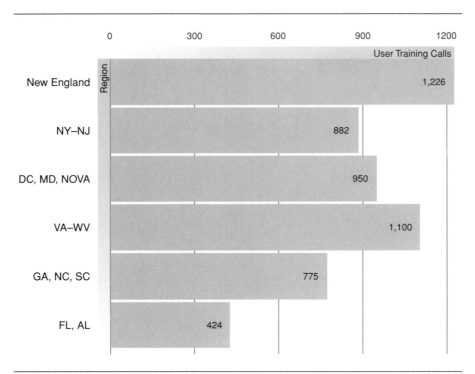

EXHIBIT 6.12 CALL TYPE NUMBER CHARTED BY TERRITORY WHEN A USER CLICKS ON THE "USER TRAINING" SLICE OF CALL-TYPE PIE CHART IN EXHIBIT 6.11

East: Hosted Apps CRM

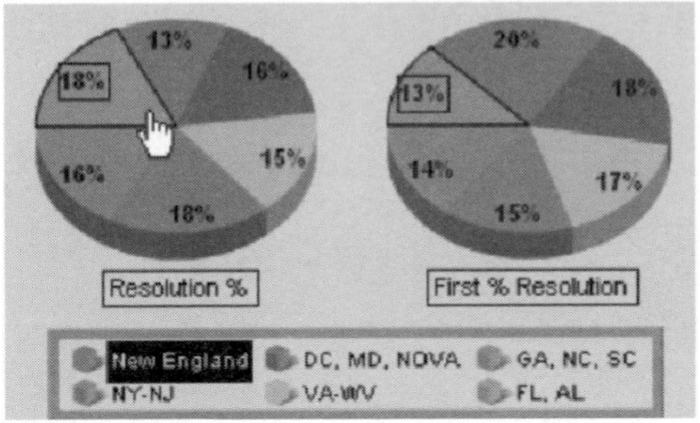

Territory	Resolution %	First % Resolution
New England	85	62
NY-NJ	65	97
DC, MD, NOVA	80	88
VA-WV	75	79
GA, NC, SC	88	72
FL, AL	78	66

EXHIBIT 6.13 RESOLUTION % AND FIRST % RESOLUTION STATISTICS BROKEN OUT BY TERRITORY FOR A MONTH WHEN USER CLICKS ON ANY GIVEN MONTH'S COLUMN FOR THE RESOLUTION % CHART FOR EAST REGION IN EXHIBIT 6.11

across all regions. Customer Service Engineers are restricted to the software group and region for which they are directly responsible. For example, a CRM Service Engineer for the East Region will not have access to East Region ERP or Central Region CRM dashboards (see Exhibit 6.11).

Note that the purpose of charts in a storyboarding template is to simply demonstrate the dashboard layouts and user navigation experience.

The two scenarios describe a step-by-step approach for the storyboarding exercise as part of a dashboard deployment. Such an exercise helps arrive at the user groups and hierarchy, dashboard groups, the privilege matrix, and also helps sketch the dashboard layout and navigation with full content (e.g., KPIs, alerts, reports, and chart types).

Having completed the storyboarding exercise, the final step is to develop, test, and deploy the real dashboards using the dashboarding software. Chapter 7 deals with the planning and teaming effort for a successful deployment.

7

PROJECT PLANNING AND BRANDING

Successful dashboard deployment is like a team sport requiring the pooling of diverse skills toward the common goal. The good part is—there's no opponent team except for a few naysayers sometimes.

Dashboard implementation demands the pooling of resources from a diverse skill set and varying areas and levels of expertise. This process requires proper coordination and project planning to ensure effective utilization of everyone's time.

The number of personnel involved in a dashboard deployment depends on the scope of a given deployment. However, a dashboard deployment is most definitely not a task that can be accomplished exclusively by the information technology (IT) department. Although IT personnel play a crucial role, it is essential that subject matter experts (SMEs) and analysts be part of any dashboarding team.

The following is a typical mix of resources and expertise required in a dashboarding team:

- Dashboard software expert
- Business intelligence expert
- Business analyst
- Department/Business Unit SME
- Database administrator
- IT manager
- Project manager

Note that in certain instances, a single individual may have two domains of the required expertise. For example, if an internal staff member has acquired dashboard software expertise through training, it is possible that the same person may also have the business analyst or business intelligence expertise for the organization. However, in larger organizations, it is much more likely that separate individuals or groups of individuals would contribute to one area of expertise.

The extent of the involvement of the various resources listed would vary depending on the phase of deployment. However, it is recommended that all team members be actively involved and informed of the weekly progress throughout the implementation phase. If each member, representing different areas of expertise, is not closely involved in each stage of the dashboard deployment process, there is a risk of building in shortcomings that may not be detected early enough during the dashboard design process.

For example, if the dashboards are being developed for the sales organization in absence of an SME in field sales reporting, the team may come to a conclusion that monthly gross sales numbers against quota need to be displayed on each regional dashboard. However, it may actually be more important that field sales managers find out net sales (less returns) because the sales force compensation is linked to the net sales and not gross sales. This small deviation in information priority may require a great deal of rework later, especially when an outsourced vendor tracks returns and its database is separate.

An early understanding of the logistics of field sales reporting would contribute to appropriate planning so that different data sources were effectively incorporated to seamlessly arrive at the net sales numbers. In other words, the involvement of each SME and technical expert contributes to the appropriateness of the design and saves a great deal of time that would need to be spent revising a design that falls short of meeting the business requirements.

Information disconnects are unfortunately prevalent in the information biosphere of most organizations. Therefore, people tend to use their ingenuity and resourcefulness to circumvent such disconnects and end up building their own information spreadsheets and silos. In the earlier example, it is likely that the sales managers would have some arrangement with the outsourced vendor in question to receive the returns' information directly. However, a dashboard cannot casually overcome such information disconnects, and if a dashboard inherits similar shortcomings, incomplete or inaccurate information can quickly render the dashboard dysfunctional. As outlined in Chapter 1 in the SMART (i.e., **S**ynergetic, **M**onitor KPIs, **A**ccurate, **R**esponsive, **T**imely) acronym, accuracy is one of the fundamental characteristics of a dashboard that is capable of serving as a live console that can effectively manage and monitor the business. Therefore, assembling the right team and keeping each member fully involved throughout the dashboarding process is extremely important.

In addition, it is critical during the early deployment phase to enlist the assistance of a representative sample of end users to assess the full scope of their information needs and to elicit their input during the storyboarding process. During the latter half of the deployment phase, a graphic designer's input is helpful to ensure an aesthetically pleasing dashboard layout and colors. If there are existing corporate standards for the use of logos, colors, fonts, graphics, disclaimers, and copyright symbols, these must be adhered to in consultation with the marketing/corporate communications team in the organization.

PROJECT MILESTONES

Business applications, deployment size, and information complexity greatly vary across different organizations. These variables render it almost impossible to generically benchmark the individual milestones of the process and to determine the length of those milestones. For example, for a small group of senior management, it may be possible to have dashboards deployed within a ten-day period. On the other extreme, an enterprise-wide deployment may take six months or longer to deploy to thousands of users. The complexity and duration of the dashboarding process depends largely on the match between the dashboarding needs, software capabilities, and the state of supporting databases.

Despite the variations in dashboard deployments, most deployments end up requiring a relative effort that falls within a similar range. Therefore, it is reasonable and useful to estimate time proportions for the different milestones applying to *most* dashboard deployments. The table in Exhibit 7.1 illustrates the milestones and corresponding effort estimates for a typical process.

Note that the estimated percentages apply against total man-hours and not to the absolute length of the project. For example, a project manager's time would be spread across the entire span of project execution, consuming an estimated 15% to 20% of total man-hours. Depending on the team composition, it is likely that a 100 man-day estimate may be completed in less than 30 working days.

A best-case scenario in which all milestones were achieved within the lower bounds of the estimate would see goals achieved within 90% of the estimated effort. On the flip side, the estimate may be extended by 10%. The absolute value of the man-hours that equates to 100% is the unknown variable that needs to be addressed on a case-by-case basis, depending on the scope of dashboard deployment and the software efficiency in accomplishing the business requirements.

Project Scoping and Branding		10%
Meta-information Gathering	Chapter 2	15 – 20%
Audience Profiling	Chapter 3	5%
System Alerts Definitions	Chapter 5	10 – 15%
Storyboarding	Chapter 6	10%
Dashboard Development	Chapters 2 – 7	25 – 30%
Testing & Final Deployment		10%
Overall Project Management		15 – 20%
TOTAL		90 – 110%

EXHIBIT 7.1 TYPICAL PROJECT MILESTONES FOR DASHBOARDING AND ESTIMATED EFFORT RELATIVE TO THE ENTIRE PROJECT

The relative estimate for each milestone outlined in Exhibit 7.1 must be taken as a general guideline. Those proportions need to be evaluated in light of each individual situation, and estimates must be adjusted accordingly.

PREREQUISITE

The milestones deal exclusively with the dashboard deployment and not with any database work that may be necessary to successfully deploy dashboards. A good deal of so-called grunt work consisting of cleansing, formatting, extracting, transforming, and loading all of the required data into a compliant database format is required before any successful dashboard deployment. Time and effort estimates for assuring the prerequisite readiness for dashboard deployment vary greatly in each situation and are outside the scope of this discussion. However, for the success of any dashboarding project, it is crucial that the dashboard team has access to the expert resources that accurately assess and estimate the time and effort involved in preparing for a dashboard deployment.

PROJECT MANAGEMENT

Good principles of project management apply to dashboarding to the same degree that they apply to any other project. Any of the various available project management methodologies may be followed: the Waterfall method, the Rapid Application Development (RAD) approach, Project Management Institute (PMI) methodology, the Capability Maturity Model (CMM) for software, or the best practices for project management recommended within the organization. In any approach, the key success factors for managing a dashboarding project are as follows:

- Early involvement of end users
- Right composition of the dashboarding team (described earlier in this chapter)
- Collaboration within the dashboarding team
- Timely readiness of the prerequisite data formats
- Appropriate selection of the dashboarding software

For larger deployments (exceeding 500 dashboard users), it is best to split the implementation process into smaller phases rather than undertaking a grand implementation approach in which the entire deployment is launched at once to all users. A phased approach may not have the big-bang dramatic effect of fulfilling the entire organization's information needs all at once, as is frequently favored with portal launches, but a phased execution assures a stepwise success, solicits early user feedback, and provides the opportunity to learn and improve on each execution phase.

Another important project management consideration is the containment of typical pitfalls that tend to lead to scope creep and unexpected project delays. As the dashboard deployment enters into its later stages, users may decide that they want dashboard design changes that they could not envision and articulate earlier. This creates a conflict between the competing goals of timely execution and a final deliverable that best meets users' expectations. However, in the interest of successful execution, it is better to defer the user enhancement request in the interest of timeliness while keeping track of all such change requirements needed for future revision.

Like any other complex project, a great deal depends on conducting proper due diligence upfront. Appropriate project scoping and planning (the first step in Exhibit 7.1) is critical and saves a great deal of time and revision throughout the process. In this stage, it is prudent to involve the expertise of an individual with experience deploying dashboards of a similar scale and complexity, using the specific software chosen. Such experience is handy in giving the team a sense of what to expect in a given deployment scope and helping to organize time and resources accordingly.

USER TRAINING

If the dashboard application requires user training, such training must be planned in a timely manner in conjunction with the release of the dashboard application. The project milestones, as outlined earlier in the chapter, do not include user training. Depending on the dashboard software, different types of user training may be required. The three common distinctions among user groups requiring different types of user training are the following:

1. Regular end users
2. Power users
3. Software administrators (typically on the IT side)

Well-designed dashboard software may not require training for regular end users or even for power users. The application, if well designed, should be intuitive enough for users to easily find the information they need. User self-help may be provided through online help documentation and mouse-over prompts.

Because all leading dashboard software programs are Web-based, the benchmark of a user-friendly application is any of the leading travel or auction portals. None of them requires user training. They are intuitive enough for regular users to get what they need, and they provide sufficient online instruction for power users who are interested in leveraging the applications' advanced capabilities. A well-designed dashboard must meet this benchmark of user-friendliness without depriving the user of its full potential to serve relevant and required information. Good dashboarding software must provide built-in personalization (content security and relevance), powerful visualization, alerts, drill-downs, and intuitive navigation.

For a large deployment with a dispersed user base, it is efficient to have a *webinar* (Web-based seminar) or an interactive tutorial that covers all key features of the dashboard. Such a webinar or interactive tutorial may be pre-recorded and made accessible through the Web or electronically distributed to all dashboard users.

BRANDING

Branding is a term borrowed from the marketing field. Branding is the process of image building for a product, service, or organization to associate a distinctive identity with the brand's name or mark.

Branding in the context of a dashboard implies developing a name (and preferably a mark or logo) for the envisioned dashboard application such that people may identify the project with that name and mark.

In my experience, branding helps marshal early recognition and support for a dashboarding effort. As described earlier, dashboarding is a team-oriented and collaborative effort and, without exception, it gets the attention of senior management. Having a brand (a relevant name and a distinguishing mark) makes communication about the project much easier within the organization. With a brand, the team members can more easily identify with the project, which creates a positive association between individuals and the project. And, it could not hurt to celebrate the successful launch of the dashboarding application with a giveaway that has the project brand as its insignia.

Like any other brand-developing exercise, the project's brand name and mark should reinforce a positive and relevant impression about the envisioned application. A brainstorming session with the business stakeholders, including someone with appropriate marketing experience, would help. Often, a creative designer who has experience developing logos could help create a strong brand mark. At the same time, there is no need to cause project delays by making the branding process too elaborate, time consuming, or expensive. Establishing a brand early on usually only requires a small initiative on the part of the project lead. Once the brand is created, it needs only a quick blessing from the senior management responsible, and the team can move on. Exhibit 7.2 shows a set of proposed logos for a branding exercise on a dashboard project.

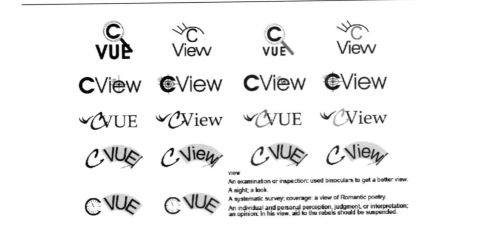

EXHIBIT 7.2 A BRANDING AND LOGO EXERCISE FOR A DASHBOARDING PROJECT THAT FOCUSED ON CUSTOMER INFORMATION

Courtesy: Lisa Dion, Art Director, WIT, www.witinc.com

PART TWO

DASHBOARD TYPES

8

DASHBOARD CATEGORIES

Enterprise dashboard applications may be as diverse and numerous as the challenges organizations face for their strategic, operational, and competitive success.

Considering the myriad applications of dashboards within organizations, dashboards may be grouped into the following major categories:

- Enterprise performance dashboards
- Divisional dashboards
- Process/activity monitoring dashboards
- Application dashboards
- Customer dashboards
- Vendor dashboards

ENTERPRISE PERFORMANCE DASHBOARDS

Enterprise performance dashboards consolidate data from various divisions and business segments and provide a holistic view of the enterprise. Such dashboards are mostly for senior management within the company.

Enterprise performance dashboards may contain the corporate financial numbers, regulatory checks such as required by corporate compliance laws, supply chain insight, sales performance by region, and key performance indicators (KPIs) for the various business segments within the company. A dashboard that consolidates all of these elements into a few dashboard screens with drill-down into further details within each area would qualify as an enterprise performance dashboard.

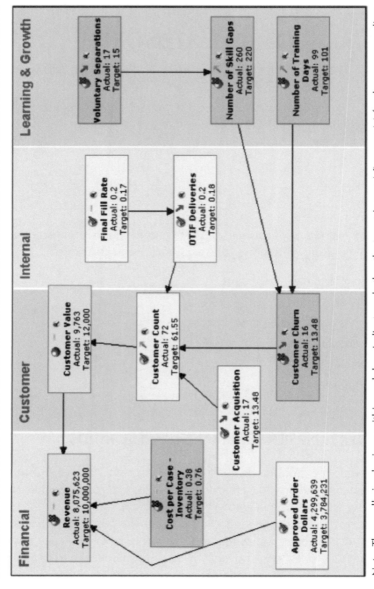

Note: The small circular icon within each box indicates whether the target is met (✓) or not (✗) for the corresponding metric. Also, an arrow next to it indicates the trend as compared to the previous period of reference for that metric.

EXHIBIT 8.1 AN ENTERPRISE PERFORMANCE DASHBOARD DISPLAYING A HIGH-LEVEL OVERVIEW OF KEY AREAS WITHIN THE ORGANIZATION AS PER THE BALANCED SCORECARD FRAMEWORK

Courtesy: Business Objects

A popular methodology for measuring organizational performance is the Balanced Scorecard developed by Robert Kaplan and David Norton.[1] Often, the enterprise management dashboard adopts the Balanced Scorecard framework, as illustrated in Exhibits 8.1 and 8.2, and allows drill-down to the details on each area of measurement.

Exhibits 8.1 and 8.2 show the high-level metrics for the four organizational perspectives as defined by the Balanced Scorecard: (1) financial, (2) customer, (3) internal process, and (4) learning and growth.

For organizations with a large and diverse corporate structure, the enterprise dashboard may be deployed at each of their strategic business units (SBUs). SBUs represent different business and operational areas within a large organization, each with significant autonomy and separation. Furthermore, each SBU has its own operational divisions, such as Sales, Marketing, Finance, Distribution, Customer Service, and so forth (see Exhibit 8.3).

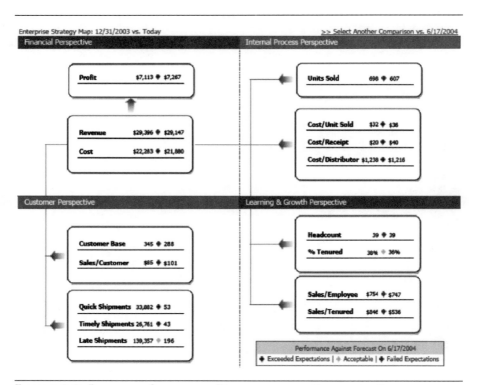

EXHIBIT 8.2 BALANCED SCORECARD DASHBOARD FOR ENTERPRISE PERFORMANCE MANAGEMENT

Courtesy: MicroStrategy

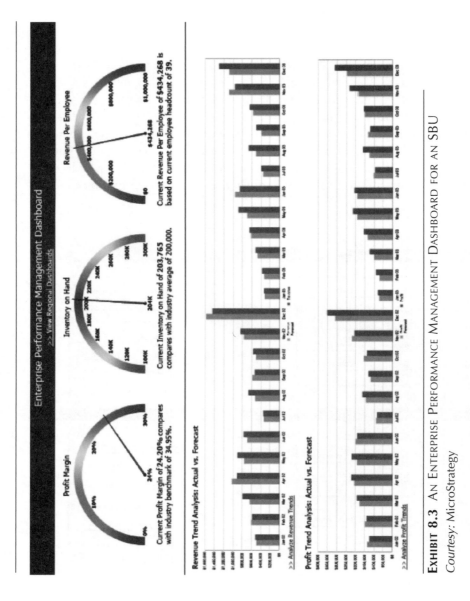

Exhibit 8.3 An Enterprise Performance Management Dashboard for an SBU

Courtesy: MicroStrategy

For example, General Electric (GE) has several SBUs, including GE Advanced Materials, GE Healthcare, GE Transportation, GE Consumer Finance, GE Commercial Finance, GE Insurance, GE Energy, NBC Universal, and so forth. Each of these SBUs has several divisions of its own.

DIVISIONAL DASHBOARDS

Divisional heads and operational managers require dashboards that display performance metrics and numbers specific to their areas of responsibility. For example, a Director of Sales for a specific business unit would want the current period unit and dollar sales within the business unit, comparisons with the same period a year ago, current trend, sales numbers by Region, top X customers by Region, number of new customers versus those who dropped out, and so forth (see Exhibit 8.4).

The following list includes the key areas of divisional dashboards:

- Sales dashboards
- Marketing dashboards
- Finance dashboards
- Supply chain dashboards
- Human resources dashboards
- Operations dashboards
- Manufacturing dashboards
- Quality control dashboards
- Purchasing dashboards

Divisional dashboards are required to support a large user base as an organization decides to roll out dashboards wider and deeper within the organization. More than 50% of the organization may have access to divisional dashboards, as dashboards are deployed across various levels within the organization.

Chapter 9 is dedicated to the subject of divisional dashboards, with examples of their diverse applications and management capabilities. A discussion of divisional dashboards provides insight into the application of dashboards at various operational levels within the enterprise.

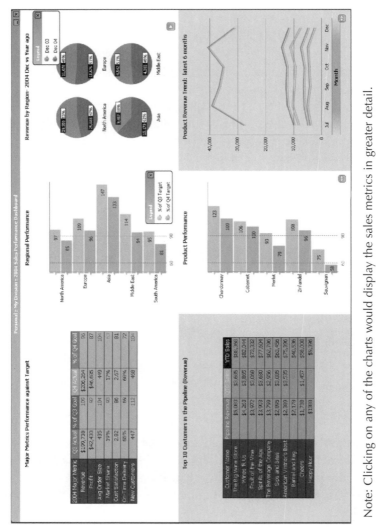

Note: Clicking on any of the charts would display the sales metrics in greater detail.

EXHIBIT 8.4 SALES DASHBOARD DISPLAYING KEY SALES METRICS FOR A DIVISION

Courtesy: iDashboards

PROCESS/ACTIVITY MONITORING DASHBOARDS

Dashboards may be deployed to monitor specific business processes or widespread activities, such as weather patterns, national security, disease control, and so on. Such dashboards may be leveraged across different departments within the organization or could be confined to a specific group responsible for monitoring certain processes or activities and informing those affected by such activities.

A visually effective and analytically equipped monitoring dashboard helps avert a problem before it becomes a real problem and attains crisis proportions. Examples of process/activity monitoring include the following:

- Fraud monitoring
- Manufacturing process monitoring
- Assembly-line monitoring
- Warehouse/distribution monitoring
- Computing resource utilization monitoring
- National/regional security monitoring
- Financial market monitoring
- Weather/climate monitoring
- Electrical grid monitoring
- Traffic monitoring

Fraud monitoring dashboards may be deployed by credit card companies and financial institutions that require proactive monitoring of potentially fraudulent transactions and identity theft cases. Large e-commerce sites may also use such dashboards to monitor excessive and unusual buying patterns to alert for identity fraud.

Manufacturing process monitoring dashboards may be deployed in factories, refineries, heavy mills, and mines to monitor their complex and critical industrial processes. Visual indicators of process flow and key point measurements within the process displayed on a dashboard and coupled with an audiovisual alerter help in active process monitoring.

Assembly-line monitoring dashboards may be deployed in assembly plants (e.g., automotive, aerospace, machinery, electronics, computers) to monitor real-time throughput and the status of assembly lines. Sensors continually sending measurement data to a dashboard with analytic capabilities help provide real-time performance of the assembly lines (see Exhibit 8.5).

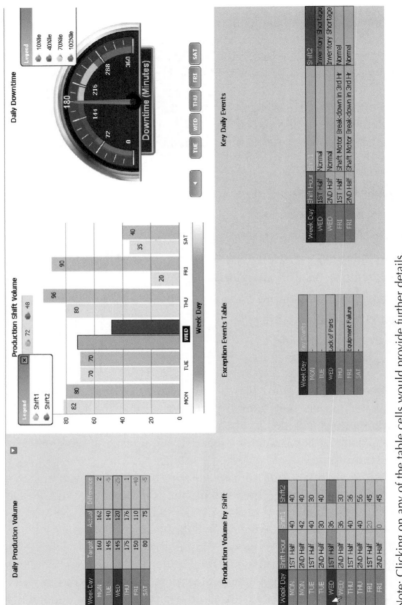

Note: Clicking on any of the table cells would provide further details.

Exhibit 8.5 Activity Monitoring Dashboard Displaying Key Metrics for Daily Shifts in a Manufacturing Assembly Plant

Courtesy: iDashboards

Warehouse/distribution monitoring dashboards may be deployed in warehouses and distribution centers to monitor real-time inventory, out-of-stock, in-transit inventory, and space allocations. Inventory analysis coupled with advanced visualization and alerts help sustain a fast-response replenishment system.

Computing resource utilization monitoring dashboards may help monitor CPU, network traffic, and disk utilization as on-demand computing grows in popularity as a preferred mode of IT resource management within organizations. Chief Technology Officers (CTOs), IT managers, and database and server administrators use such dashboards as live windows into the computer systems they are responsible to support and upkeep with a minimum performance guarantee.

National/regional security monitoring dashboards may help monitor new patterns of unexpected disease outbreaks (symptoms of chemical or biological attacks), unexpected viral strains with epidemic hazards, and so on.

Financial market monitoring dashboards may help monitor live financial market conditions, macroeconomic indicators, stocks and bonds trading, commodity trading, news feeds, and analyses. Most fund managers and serious traders use some type of financial monitoring dashboard to keep up with the dynamic nature of financial markets and the multitude of variables in play at any given time.

Weather and climate monitoring dashboards may help track weather patterns across certain regions and monitor climate trends.

Electrical grid monitoring dashboards may help monitor power distribution, consumption, and power failures throughout various parts of a complex electrical distribution system. Especially in situations where power demand exceeds supply, such monitoring is critical to perform load balancing and develop distribution schemes (blackout management).

Traffic monitoring dashboards may help in monitoring traffic patterns, congestion, and needs analysis for road network, subway system, rail network, and air traffic. Such dashboards are leveraged by transportation and traffic agencies to proactively alleviate delays, respond to crises, and plan improvements (see Exhibit 8.6).

APPLICATION DASHBOARDS

Application dashboards are mostly embedded within custom applications to provide specific metrics defined within the application. Application dashboards could be as diverse as the custom applications and may be defined by

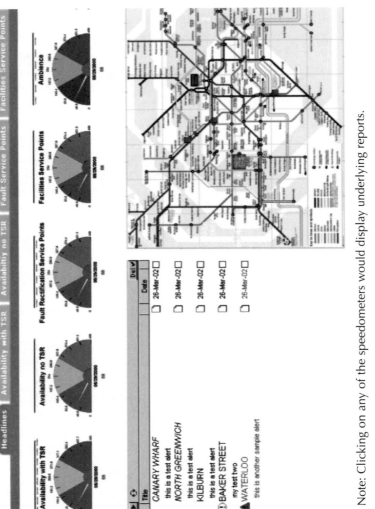

Note: Clicking on any of the speedometers would display underlying reports.

EXHIBIT 8.6 ACTIVITY MONITORING DASHBOARD DISPLAYING KEY METRICS FOR A METRO SYSTEM

Courtesy: Business Objects

the application vendor or the application team responsible for developing the custom application.

The following is a sample of custom applications with embedded dashboards:

- Workflow management
- Asset management
- Travel management
- Risk management
- Quality audit management
- Commodity trading
- Bio-informatics analysis

Application dashboards often become the preferred user interface for the application and facilitate user interaction with the underlying application.

CUSTOMER DASHBOARDS

Customer dashboards are for the use of the customers of an organization. They are outward-facing dashboards with metrics relevant to the customers of an organization.

Business-to-consumer (B2C) companies dealing directly with end consumers may deploy individual customer dashboards. For example, utility, phone, and cable companies, banks, credit cards, and online trading companies may deploy dashboards with metrics dealing with individual customer transactions.

Business-to-business (B2B) companies dealing with business customers may deploy business account dashboards. For example, office suppliers, computer manufacturers, and commercial travel agencies may deploy account-level dashboards for their business customers to track and manage company-wide purchases. Service outsourcing companies may deploy customer dashboards for their customers to monitor service-level agreements and track the KPIs for performed outsourced services. For a global customer, such dashboards may be customized to provide regional metrics as per the customer's regional organization and management hierarchy.

Exhibit 8.7 provides an example of a marketing agency deploying a dashboard for its customers to monitor the response for their various marketing campaigns.

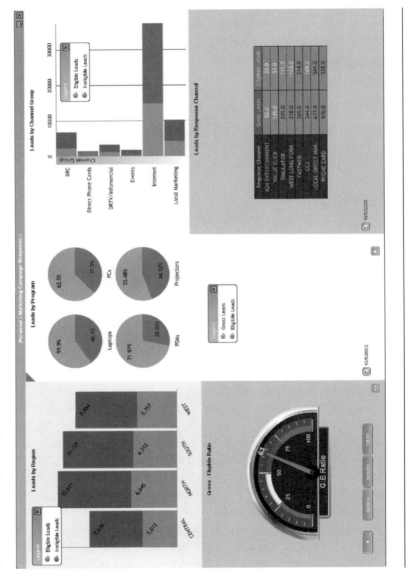

EXHIBIT 8.7 MARKETING AGENCY DASHBOARD WITH LIVE STATUS ON DIFFERENT MARKETING CAMPAIGNS BY REGION FOR A GIVEN CUSTOMER

Courtesy: iDashboards

Michael Hammer, the best-selling author of *Reengineering the Corporation,*[2] discusses the pressing need for organizations to collaborate with their customers and vendors and achieve virtual integration (not vertical integration). From his best-selling book, *The Agenda: What Every Business Must Do to Dominate the Decade,*[3] the following are a few of the many agenda items that he lays out for an organization to succeed:

- Streamline the connections between your processes and those of your customers and suppliers.
- Exploit the opportunity of collaborating with co-customers and co-suppliers.
- See your business not as a self-contained company but as part of an extended enterprise of companies that work together to create customer value.

In order to create such virtual integration between the company and its vendors, vendor dashboards may be deployed as a communication platform with added value for vendors.

VENDOR DASHBOARDS

Vendor dashboards allow vendors to collaborate and keep abreast of the details regarding their interaction with an organization. For example, a large automotive manufacturer may have a supplier dashboard for its automotive parts vendors to monitor the supply chain, product requirements, purchase orders, and service-level agreements. Some of the KPIs for vendor dashboards may include vendor-specific performance benchmarks, aggregated metrics from other vendors, vendor advisory, vendor quality audits, quality metrics, business volume, and financial metrics.

Vendor dashboards could be an effective value-added service in vendor relationships. When each vendor can measure its performance against an expected benchmark, as well as against other vendors, it helps provide an active feedback with measurable metrics to the vendor regarding its products and services. Vendor dashboards may be an integral part of a vendor portal, which may serve as the organizational front to manage vendor relationships (note the difference between portal and dashboard as defined in Chapter 1).

Exhibit 8.8 provides a comprehensive framework of the different dashboard categories as described in this chapter, and expanded upon further into the next chapter.

Dashboard Categories

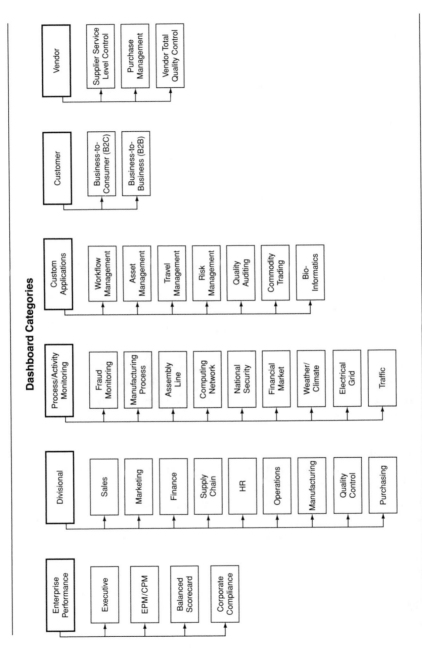

EXHIBIT 8.8 A FRAMEWORK OF DASHBOARD CATEGORIES THAT SUMMARIZES THE DIVERSE APPLICATIONS OF ENTERPRISE DASHBOARDS

ENDNOTES

1. Robert Kaplan and David Norton, "The Balanced Scorecard: Measures That Drive Performance," *Harvard Business Review* (January–February 1992).
2. Michael Hammer and James Champy, *Reengineering the Corporation: A Manifesto for Business Revolution* (New York: HarperBusiness, 2001).
3. Michael Hammer, *The Agenda: What Every Business Must Do to Dominate the Decade* (Three Rivers, MI: Three Rivers Press, 2003).

9

DIVISIONAL DASHBOARDS

Each division (or department) deserves specialized dashboards that best serve its operational needs and performance monitoring.

Divisional (or departmental) dashboards serve the specific needs of a division or department within a large organization. For example, the information needs of the Sales department are very different from those of Human Resources or Supply Chain. Therefore, deployment of divisional dashboards requires focus and subject matter expertise from the specific department the dashboards would serve.

The following are some of the broad categories for divisional dashboards:

- Sales dashboards
- Marketing dashboards
- Finance dashboards
- Supply chain dashboards
- Customer service dashboards
- Human resources dashboards
- Manufacturing dashboards
- Operations dashboards
- Quality control dashboards
- Purchasing dashboards

Design and content of a divisional dashboard must reflect the performance metrics and business organization for the specific division within the organization. The rest of this chapter provides illustrative examples for each divisional dashboard, assuming a scenario in each case. It also provides some of the commonly prevailing key performance indicators (KPIs) for each of the divisions.

SALES

Sales dashboards contain all relevant metrics required for sales management. The metrics would be aggregated at the level of an individual's responsibility. The following are some of the sales metrics that may be covered within a sales dashboard:

- Regional and territorial sales by product
- Actual versus forecast
- Sales funnel and pipeline
- Sales quota versus actual (aggregated and by sales representative)
- Sales by customer
- Inactive customer tracking
- Channel sales
- Sales promotional calendar
- Promotional response analysis
- Shipments by delivery status

Sales Division Scenario

There are four regions, and under each region there are several geographic sections to be managed. The product is divided into various categories. Regional sales managers require the sales quota and actual sales numbers for the overall region, as well as for each of the sections within their region in various categories. They also require different category scorecards for their regions as well as alerts when certain metrics go out of acceptable ranges.

The design of an effective dashboard in this scenario would require application of appropriate chart types such as trend line, pie charts, and bar charts. For example, the past three to six months of sales could be represented through a trend line; pie charts would indicate the monthly aggregated contributions of various product categories, stacked charts would show relative contributions by the sections within a region, and column charts would compare current versus year-ago numbers for the various product categories as well as for the sections within the region (see Exhibit 9.1; note that a user could then drill down into any given category to get more sales trend for that category).

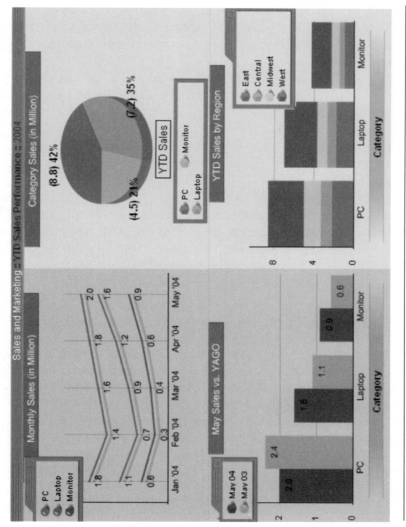

EXHIBIT 9.1 YEAR-TO-DATE (YTD) SALES PERFORMANCE DASHBOARD AT PRODUCT CATEGORY LEVEL

Courtesy: iDashboards

Each of these charts in the exhibit should also be clickable to drill down into more detailed charts and reports. For example, clicking on a slice of the Category Sales pie chart could lead to a trend line for the past 6 to 12 months of sales (units and dollars) for that category (see Exhibits 9.2 and 9.3). Furthermore, each point on the trend line could lead to a report that provides numbers at a lower aggregate level of time. For example, clicking on a specific month on the trend line could lead to the report with daily or weekly numbers for that month while maintaining the context (specific category that a user clicked on).

Another aspect of a sales dashboard that is helpful to a regional manager would be the ability to look at individual states and metro areas within the region (see Exhibit 9.4).

Note that a user could then drill down into any given state to get the relevant metrics for metro areas or any other territorial breaks within the state. Color can be used to indicate the relative performance against preset benchmarks for the respective metrics.

Speedometer chart types could be applied to contrast quota versus actual sales numbers for the sections and categories. Clicking on a given area of the chart could then lead to a more detailed report. Also, regional maps could be transposed with threshold-driven color-coded metrics for better visualization of various states within the region and also to show their comparative performance at a glance. For example, Exhibit 9.4 shows average unit price and monthly sales for the state of Arizona. The different color shades also indicate the relative performance of each of the two metrics for Arizona.

Finally, alerts could be built on each of the categories within sections. If the sales unit or dollar go below or above predefined thresholds for each of the section-category segments within a region, an alert would be visually presented on the regional dashboard. Moreover, clicking on such an alert could link to a more detailed chart or report about the alerted section.

The aforementioned dashboard could also be extrapolated to lower levels of sales management, all the way down to the individual sales representatives to help them track their individual performance against the corporate benchmark.

Another function of a sales dashboard could be to monitor aspects of the sales process, such as sales funnel analysis and collaboration among the organizational staff responsible for a territory (see Exhibit 9.5).

Note that the lower half of the dashboard provides a collaborative platform on which to communicate about relevant issues with other team members who hold similar dashboard privileges.

(text continues on page 121)

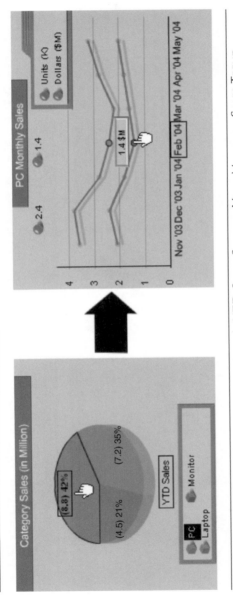

EXHIBIT 9.2 DRILL DOWN ON ANY CATEGORY'S YTD SALES SLICE TO VIEW MONTHLY SALES TREND

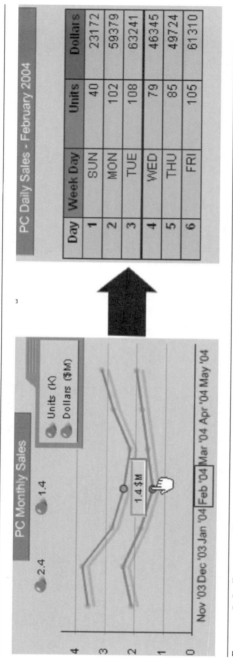

EXHIBIT 9.3 FURTHER DRILL DOWN AT CATEGORY LEVEL MONTH SALES TO VIEW DAILY/WEEKLY SALES METRICS

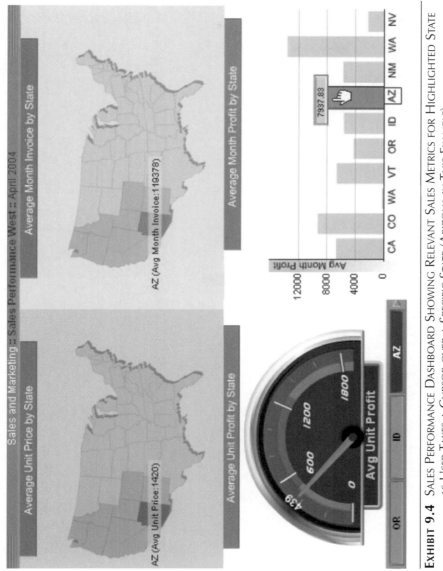

EXHIBIT 9.4 SALES PERFORMANCE DASHBOARD SHOWING RELEVANT SALES METRICS FOR HIGHLIGHTED STATE AS USER TAKES A CURSOR OVER A SPECIFIC STATE (ARIZONA IN THIS EXAMPLE)

119

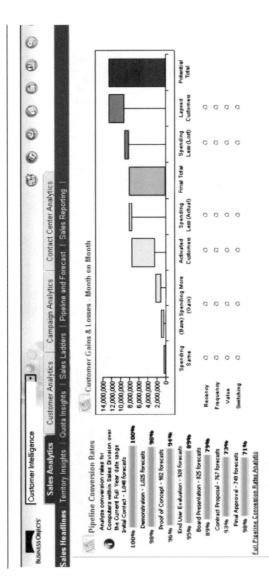

EXHIBIT 9.5 SALES ANALYTICS DASHBOARD DISPLAYING KEY SALES METRICS FOR AN ORGANIZATION

Courtesy: Business Objects

A user may click on any of the tabs and subtabs on the dashboard's *landing page* (the first screen that loads for the dashboard) to navigate to other areas. For example, clicking on the Sales Reporting tab in Exhibit 9.5 provides access to a collection of sales reports. The Pipeline and Forecast tab may provide access to a product-level forecast compared against the sales pipeline for the current month and the quarter.

MARKETING

A marketing dashboard contains all relevant metrics required by the Marketing department. Typical marketing metrics might include current marketing campaigns, media purchase, promotional effectiveness, budget versus expenditure, Web page traffic metrics, insight into competitive landscape, pricing, cross-buying analysis, as well as industry trend summaries.

Metrics would be presented depending on the area of an individual's responsibility within marketing. The following are some of the metrics that may be included in a marketing dashboard:

- Promotional campaign
- Marketing budget versus spending
- Marketing programs by region and territory
- Web trends and click-stream analysis
- Market shares
- Product mix and cross buying
- Pricing elasticity
- Product basket analysis
- Product propensity analysis
- Sales and market share trends
- Promotions versus sales
- Industry trends and external influences to sales

Marketing Division Scenario

Interactive marketing is a separate area that deals with companies' Web sites. It is responsible for Web traffic metrics for the various Web properties as well as for online marketing campaigns. Therefore, the Director of Interactive Marketing requires the weekly trend of Web traffic metrics for each of the different sections of the Web site (the company markets various types of automobiles). Also, metrics are required for weekly purchase of online impressions through search engines and relevant Web sites that have sold online banner advertising. Furthermore, the dashboard must show a summary of noninteractive marketing campaigns, which include TV, radio, trade shows, magazine advertisements, and so on.

The design of an effective dashboard in this scenario would require the application of appropriate chart types such as trend line, pie charts, column charts, and bubble charts. For example, the past three to six months of Web traffic broken out by Web properties could be represented through a trend line chart. Column charts would indicate the weekly aggregated contributions of originating Web traffic by key referral sites such as Google, Yahoo, and other popular sites where banner advertising has been launched. Pie charts would indicate the Web traffic numbers broken out by brand or vehicle group that make up the various sections on the company's Web sites (see Exhibit 9.6).

Bubble charts could be applied to present, at a glance, the relationship between traffic generated, money invested, and leads generated by each of the popular public Web sites through which an online campaign was launched. Leads generated could be represented through the bubble size on the chart to immediately show the most effective and least effective campaigns. Each of the bubbles would then be clickable to show the weekly traffic generation from that specific Web site.

Metrics for the noninteractive marketing campaigns could be presented through a summarized table. Each of the table rows or cells could then be clicked to drill down to get more details on a certain campaign type.

Finally, alerts could be built on each of the campaigns as well as on Web traffic thresholds. When a new marketing campaign is introduced, an alert would display. Clicking on the visual alert would provide descriptive details about that campaign. Web traffic alerts for each of the Web sites and brand sections thereof would lead to e-mail alerts when Web traffic metrics go out of the predefined threshold limits. Clicking on such alerts would display line charts showing the Web traffic trend for the specific Web site or brand section.

Another perspective for a marketing dashboard would be to analyze cross-buying behavior. This would help develop targeted promotions with higher effectiveness. Exhibit 9.7 indicates an analytic dashboard that combines pricing with cross-buying behavior among different segments of computer and related peripherals. Note that the dashboard in this example

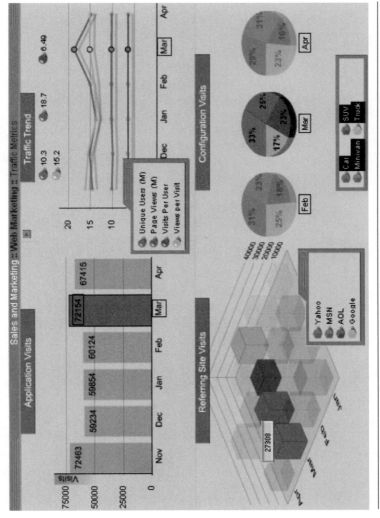

EXHIBIT 9.6 MARKETING DASHBOARD DISPLAYING WEB SITE TRAFFIC METRICS FOR AN AUTO-MOTIVE WEB SITE

Courtesy: iDashboards

123

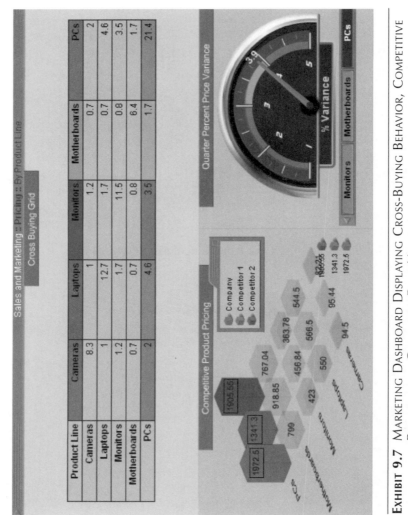

EXHIBIT 9.7 MARKETING DASHBOARD DISPLAYING CROSS-BUYING BEHAVIOR, COMPETITIVE PRICING, AND QUARTERLY PRICE VARIANCE

Courtesy: iDashboards

combines data from an external marketing research vendor that tracks competitive pricing.

FINANCE

A finance dashboard contains all relevant metrics for the Chief Financial Officer (CFO) and the Finance and Accounting areas. Typical finance metrics could include current sales by various geographic regions and business units, cost of sales, accounts receivable and payable, cash flow, profit and loss (P&L), cost center, budget versus actual, as well as regulatory compliance metrics.

Depending on the level and area of an individual's responsibility, the metrics would be presented for that area at appropriate aggregate levels with security to block nonprivileged metrics. The following are some of the financial areas that may be included within a finance dashboard:

- *Financial statements.* Income sheet, balance sheet, and cash flow
- *Audit control.* Journal analysis and debt analysis
- *Cost control.* Departmental cost, budget versus expenses
- *Activity-based costing.* Cost centers and cost activities
- *Accounts receivable.* Collections, risks, and discount analysis
- *Accounts payable.* Cash and discount optimization, supplier data sheet
- *Expense cycle.* Aging, cash out flow, and purchase requisition
- *Revenue cycle.* Revenue ladder, funnel, and product backlog
- *Regulatory compliance and audit controls*

With strict regulatory compliance laws in effect, senior management and CFOs need help in monitoring compliance across the organization. A finance dashboard may serve as an effective console to manage compliance workflow and processes (see Exhibit 9.8).

Financial Division Scenario

An Accounts Receivables Manager across all the business units is responsible for several associates, who call in for delinquent accounts. Therefore, this manager requires the weekly trend of total receivables past the due date, with numbers further broken out by the number of days past due. He also needs to monitor these metrics by each of the associates who report directly to him. Some further performance met-

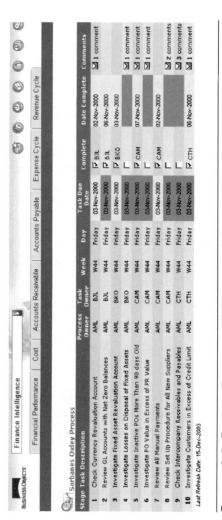

EXHIBIT 9.8 FINANCE DASHBOARD ILLUSTRATING PROCESS COLLABORATION FEATURE FOR THE SARBANES-OXLEY COMPLIANCE

Courtesy: Business Objects

rics of these associates are required, such as the weekly recovery by each of them, average maturity age of delinquent accounts assigned to each of them compared to the overall average, and so forth.

The design of an effective dashboard in this scenario would require application of appropriate chart types such as trend line, bar/column charts, and summarized reports. For example, the past three months of account receivables broken out by Web business unit could be represented through a trend line chart. Column charts would indicate the account receivables numbers broken out by each of the associates while comparing with payments received for the latest completed period. These could also be superimposed with a plot indicating the average maturity age of delinquent accounts assigned to each of the associates.

A report that summarizes the top X delinquent accounts in terms of dollars, along with the assigned associate, and top X delinquent accounts in terms of days past due may also be required. Each of the table rows or cells could then be clicked to drill down to get more details on each of those accounts as well as a potential link to a Web service that provides credit ratings.

Traffic light and thermometer chart types could be applied to highlight the aggregated performance metrics for each associate. A red traffic light chart for a given associate could indicate that his receivables percentage is lower than a certain threshold that indicates the group average. A thermometer may show the total receivables for each of the associates and also highlight their comparative performance at a glance.

Note that the key difference between a dashboard, as described, and an accounts receivable software program that may provide some of this information is the power of visualization and consolidation of all relevant metrics required for better management. An effective dashboard would ensure that a problem requiring immediate attention is not overlooked or buried under disparate reports and numbers. The enhanced information visualization capacity improves enterprise performance management at every level of the dashboard deployment.

SUPPLY CHAIN

A supply chain dashboard contains all relevant metrics for the Supply Chain department responsible for distribution, inventory, and logistics management. Typical supply chain metrics might include inventory turn, days of supply, fill rate, distribution time, in-transit inventory, rate of damaged goods, on-time delivery, gross margin, and supply chain scorecards.

Depending on the level and area of an individual's responsibility, the metrics would be presented for that area at appropriate aggregate levels with security to block nonprivileged metrics. The following are some of the supply chain areas and corresponding metrics that may be included within a dashboard:

- *Inventory.* Days of supply, inventory turns, average time to ship, % open orders
- *Cost.* Return on capital, overheads, margin
- *Transshipment.* Volume in-transit, interwarehouse shipment, loading-unloading time, % damages

---

Supply Chain Division Scenario

A Distribution Manager for the North Region requires a supply chain dashboard. This manager requires the weekly sales numbers for each item (or stock keeping unit, SKU) with variance to indicate anticipated adjustment in the inventory. The requirements include quarterly tracking of inventory turns and gross margin for the region as compared to the overall company. Also, there is a need for real-time days of supply and inventory turns for each product category with further drill-down into each item.

The design of an effective dashboard in this scenario would require application of appropriate chart types such as pie, trend line, bar/column charts, and summary tables. For example, weekly sales by SKU may be in a table format because a large number of SKUs need to be displayed. Negative variances may be highlighted in red to get a viewer's immediate attention. Quarterly inventory turn tracking may be displayed as a trend line, while the gross margin may be juxtaposed on the same time frame as a column chart with a different scale. Days of supply for different categories may be displayed as a small table, which may be drilled down to similar metrics at the individual SKU level within each category (see Exhibit 9.9).

Another useful function for a supply chain dashboard would be to monitor a scorecard in terms of percent flexibility and reliability of the distribution channel. How many delivered orders are damaged or wrongly delivered as a percentage of the total purchase orders? These metrics would indicate the efficacy of the supply chain and the performance of the people responsible. They would also be leading indicators of customer satisfaction and costs (see Exhibit 9.10).

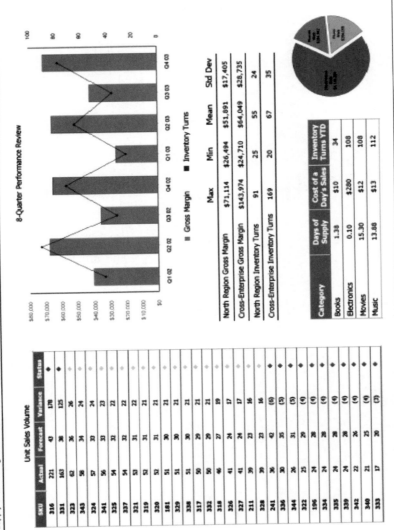

EXHIBIT 9.9 SUPPLY CHAIN DASHBOARD SHOWING KPIs FOR A SPECIFIC REGION
Courtesy: MicroStrategy

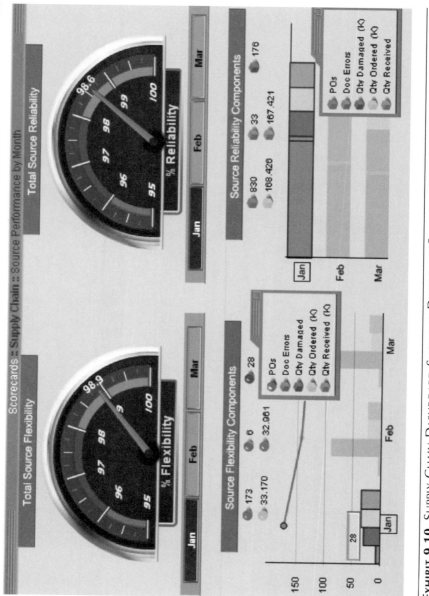

EXHIBIT 9.10 SUPPLY CHAIN DASHBOARD SHOWING DIVISIONAL SCORECARD

Courtesy: iDashboards

CUSTOMER SERVICE

A customer service dashboard contains all relevant metrics for managing customer service performance. Typical customer service metrics would include purchase cycle funnel, customer service response, problem resolution time, successful resolution percentage, customer service level agreement, and customer service scorecards.

Depending on the level and area of an individual's responsibility, the metrics would be presented for that area at appropriate aggregate levels with security to block nonprivileged metrics. The following are some of the customer service areas that may be included within a dashboard:

- Customer service support and troubleshooting
- Warranty incidents
- Customer survey and feedback
- Customer acquisition funnel, retention, and churn rate
- Order delivery and open orders
- Service-level agreements

For larger customers that place many orders and may have certain service-level agreements, an organization may provide a customer-specific dashboard that each authorized user would access to monitor the customer service level it receives, and compare this against prearranged service-level agreements. The customer may also use this dashboard to track the status of open orders, shipments, and open customer service cases.

Customer Service Scenario

A Customer Service Account Manager for an enterprise software company requires a dashboard. This manager requires the open purchase orders in a region broken out by each stage of the order delivery: order, acquisition, delivery, and software installation. The manager also needs to know a cumulative conversion rate for each order stage to ascertain the efficacy of customer service handling within each stage. Also, this requires access to delivery cycle time for each stage of the order delivery process.

The design of an effective dashboard in this scenario would require application of appropriate chart types such as stacked column and pie charts along with a speedometer chart. For example, each stage of the order delivery may be displayed through a pie chart, with order count and relative percentage in each stage. The cumulative percentage for each order stage might be portrayed using a speedometer. Delivery cycle time for each stage of the order delivery process may be displayed as a stacked column for each month (see Exhibit 9.11).

HUMAN RESOURCES

A human resources dashboard contains relevant metrics for managing the Human Resources department. Typical human resources metrics would include employee retention, employee turnover, employee training, skill gaps, headcount, travel costs, overheads, and human resources scorecards.

Depending on the level and area of an individual's responsibility, the metrics would be presented for that area at appropriate aggregate levels with security to block nonprivileged metrics. The following are some of the human resources areas that may be included within a dashboard:

- Turnovers, new hires, and layoffs
- Skill gaps and training
- Employee satisfaction surveys and feedbacks
- Per-head productivity and revenue
- Employee costs, overheads, and benefits
- Full-time, part-time, and contractors

Human Resources Dashboard Scenario

The Vice President of Human Resources requires a dashboard with headcount summary by department, broken out into segments of full-time versus overall. She requires total employee costs by each department along with a comparison of the variance against the previous year. She also requires skill gap and turnover ratio information by each department.

The design of an effective dashboard in this scenario would require application of appropriate chart types such as column and pie charts along with speedometer charts. For example, headcount summary by department may be displayed through a pie chart, with separate pie charts for full-time versus overall headcount. Employee costs and quarterly variance by each department may be shown as a combination chart (column and line charts combined), where the line shows

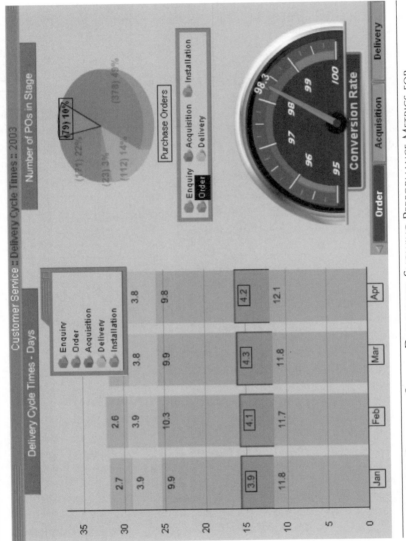

EXHIBIT 9.11 CUSTOMER SERVICE DASHBOARD SHOWING PERFORMANCE METRICS FOR THE CUSTOMER ACQUISITION FUNNEL

Courtesy: iDashboards

the variance. Skill gap and turnover ratio information may be effectively displayed on speedometers, with thresholds to indicate the relative performance of these metrics (see Exhibit 9.12). The bands within the speedometers indicate the ranges for industry averages for the corresponding metrics. This would help monitor the company's workforce satisfaction as compared to similar companies within the industry.

MANUFACTURING

A manufacturing dashboard contains relevant metrics for managing a manufacturing operation. Typical manufacturing metrics would include capital expenditures, manufacturing costs broken into cost components, production times, production batches, real-time production status, and manufacturing scorecards.

Depending on the level and area of an individual's responsibility, the metrics would be presented for that area at appropriate aggregate levels with security to block nonprivileged metrics.

Manufacturing Dashboard Scenario

The Vice President of Manufacturing requires a dashboard with manufacturing costs broken out by material cost, labor, overheads, and depreciation. He needs to monitor the monthly trend of manufacturing lead times in number of days and manufacturing batch sizes. He also requires three-month performance of capital expenditure against the budget.

The design of an effective dashboard in this scenario would require application of appropriate chart types such as stacked charts, trend line, and pie charts. For example, the material cost, labor, overheads, and depreciation metrics could be charted in a stacked bar chart. Capital expenditure could be shown as a monthly trend as compared against the budget. A trend line chart may show the manufacturing lead times trended over a three-month period and broken out in segments by the duration of manufacturing period (in days). Total manufacturing volume might be broken out by batch sizes and displayed in a pie chart to show the volume distribution by batch size (see Exhibit 9.13).

Another function of a manufacturing dashboard might be to monitor daily operations with production volume by shift, downtime, and interruption mon-

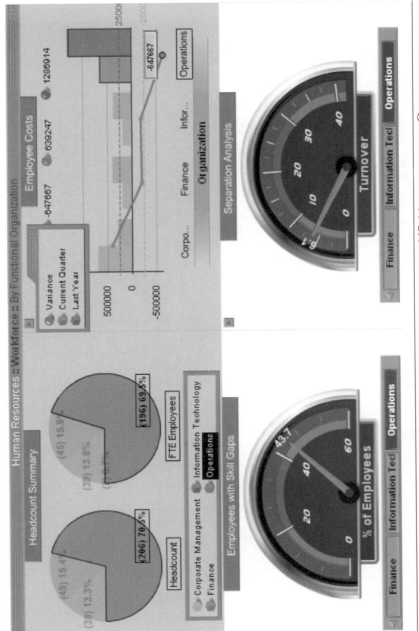

EXHIBIT 9.12 HUMAN RESOURCES DASHBOARD SHOWING AGGREGATED HR METRICS FOR THE ORGANIZATION

Courtesy: iDashboards

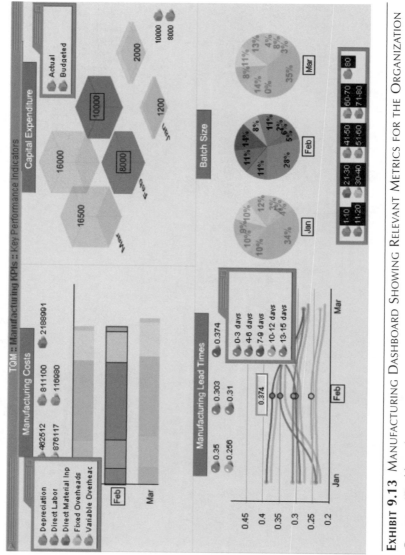

EXHIBIT 9.13 MANUFACTURING DASHBOARD SHOWING RELEVANT METRICS FOR THE ORGANIZATION

Courtesy: iDashboards

itoring. Exhibit 9.14 shows a manufacturing dashboard with operations metrics for daily shifts and a description for production line interruption, if any.

OPERATIONS MANAGEMENT

An operations management dashboard is the most diverse of all divisional dashboards. It is unique to each organization and how it manages its operations. In some ways it is similar to the enterprise performance dashboards, except that there may be a separate operations dashboard for each major area of operation within the enterprise. For example, a large retail chain may have its operations divided among stores, online, catalog, specialty, merchandising, and so forth. Each of these operations may have full-fledged departments of their own, and therefore they may not be viewed within the perspective of departments as discussed in this chapter, although these separate operations may share some common administrative departments such as Finance, Human Resources, and Order Fulfillment.

Operations management dashboards are for the senior managers responsible for the overall operations. Because the perspective of operations may widely vary by organization type, the key focus in each case must be to capture the metrics that reflect operational throughput. The following are a small sample of disparate operations types requiring operations management dashboard:

- Manufacturing and/or assembly operations
- Retail operations
- Services and consulting operations
- Call center operations
- Software development and testing operations
- Health care service operations
- Public service operations (government organizations)
- Charitable or social operations

Operations Management Dashboard Scenario

The director of a call center requires a dashboard with performance metrics for all call center staff members and the ability to compare each staff's performance against team benchmarks. She wants to view

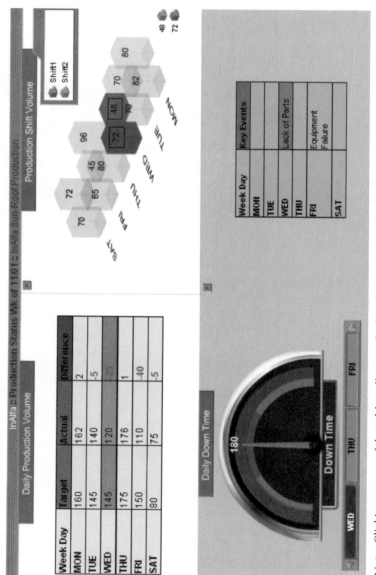

Note: Clicking on any of the table cells provides hourly production details for the two shifts during that day (see Exhibit 9.15).

EXHIBIT 9.14 ACTIVITY MONITORING DASHBOARD DISPLAYING KEY METRICS FOR DAILY SHIFTS IN A MANUFACTURING ASSEMBLY LINE

Courtesy: iDashboards

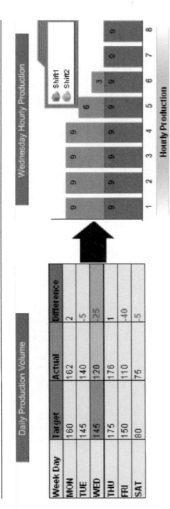

Daily Production Volume

Week Day	Target	Actual	Difference
MON	160	162	2
TUE	145	140	-5
WED	145	120	-25
THU	175	176	1
FRI	150	110	-40
SAT	80	75	-5

Wednesday Hourly Production

Note: Notice the slowdown in production during hours 5 and 6 and eventual halting during hours 7 and 8 of Shift 2.

EXHIBIT 9.15 DRILLING DOWN INTO WEDNESDAY FROM THE WEEKLY TABLE LEADS TO A DAILY CHART SHOWING BOTH SHIFTS' HOURLY PRODUCTION OUTPUT FOR THAT DAY

the weekly performance at a glance with key metrics such as number of calls handled, call handling time, and wrap-talk.

The design of an effective dashboard in this scenario would require application of appropriate chart types such as stacked column and trend line charts along with pivoting capability. For example, the talk time and wrap time may be charted as relative to each other using stacked column charts, and call volume may be charted as a separate three-dimensional column series. The individual handle time may be compared with the team's handle time as a combination chart (column and trend line combination) to easily show the relative performance of an individual as compared to the team (see Exhibit 9.16). Pivoting capability is key in an easy comparison of a given individual's performance against the team's or any other staff member with a similar type of call handling situation.

QUALITY CONTROL

Quality control dashboards help monitor quality in the different contexts of operations such as manufacturing, services, retailing, customer service, and so forth. A quality control dashboard may be applied to manage statistical process control (SPC), total quality control, or Six Sigma. The dashboard design and metrics for each situation would reflect a given organization's quality control process.

Quality control dashboards serve as valuable extensions of enterprise or operations management dashboards. The following are some of the quality control areas that may be designed within a dashboard:

- Manufacturing statistical process control
- Total quality management (TQM)
- Public sector continuous improvement
- ISO9000 and quality audit
- Returns and damage
- Six Sigma (for products, processes, and services)

Quality Control Dashboard Scenario

The Vice President of Operations for a retail chain requires a dashboard to gauge TQM within the organization. He wants to view the long-term comparison of returned goods broken out by different return

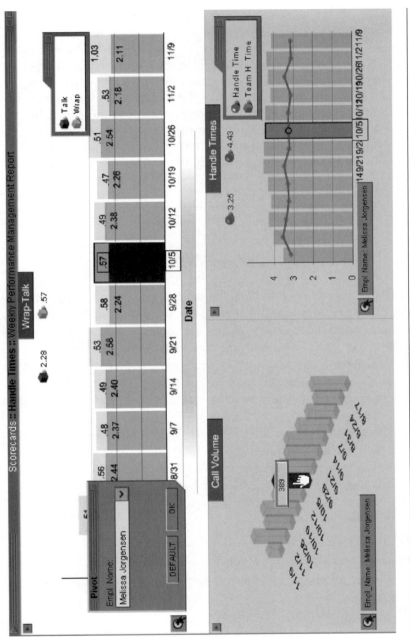

EXHIBIT 9.16 OPERATIONS MANAGEMENT DASHBOARD DISPLAYING KEY PERFORMANCE METRICS BY EMPLOYEES FOR A CALL CENTER OPERATION

Courtesy: iDashboards

reasons. He also wants to monitor monthly return value as compared with targets and the returns across the entire supply chain.

The design of an effective dashboard in this scenario would require application of appropriate chart types such as bar and trend line, and pie charts with drill-down to more detailed charts and reports. For example, monthly return values by reason may be charted as monthly trend lines for each return reason. The monthly return values for the current three months may be charted as a bar chart to easily show the relative performance with respect to the target. The returns across the supply chain pipeline may be viewed as a set of pie charts, with each pie slice representing a specific node within the supply chain. The largest pie slice would indicate the highest return at that node of the supply chain. Each month could be represented by a separate pie chart (see Exhibit 9.17).

PURCHASING

Purchasing dashboards help monitor the metrics relevant to the purchasing efficiency of the organization. Buyers responsible for making purchases may monitor their performance against individual goals as well as organizational benchmarks. They can also monitor the competitiveness of their vendor pool to best negotiate purchase discounts. Typical purchase metrics would include discount goals, outstanding budgets, expenditures, vendor volumes, discounts, top few and bottom few vendors based on purchase volume, and so forth.

Depending on the level and area of an individual's responsibility, the metrics would be presented for that area at appropriate aggregate levels with security to block nonprivileged metrics. The following are some of the purchasing areas that may be designed within a dashboard:

- Vendor quality and timeliness
- Vendor diversity goals
- Cost savings and escalations (benchmarked against budgets)
- Pricing, job estimates, and customer service alerts (affected by cost changes)
- Vendor discount factors
- Purchasing funnel (request for quote, bidding, evaluation, purchase orders, delivery, and payments)

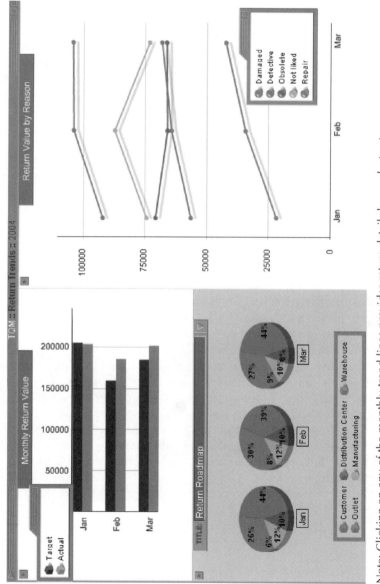

Note: Clicking on any of the monthly trend lines provides return details by product category.

EXHIBIT 9.17 QUALITY CONTROL DASHBOARD DISPLAYING KEY METRICS REFLECTING QUALITY ISSUES BY MONTH AND A THREE-YEAR PERSPECTIVE

Note that the term *vendor* as implied here may be interchanged with *supplier* or *partner*, depending on the terminology used within the organization.

Purchasing Dashboard Scenario

A senior buyer within a multinational manufacturing company is responsible for all of the computer hardware and software purchases. He needs a dashboard to monitor the monthly requests by IT and various other departments, the allocated budget, vendor bids, and purchases. He also needs to track negotiated discounts from original bids and the proportion of purchase amount to attain a minimum corporate mandate of 20% of all purchases obtained through minority-owned small businesses. Furthermore, he needs to track the fiscal year purchases as compared to the overall budget broken out by new hardware, software, and upgrades.

The design of an effective dashboard in this scenario would require application of appropriate chart types such as column and trend line, and pie charts with drill-down to more detailed charts and reports. For example, monthly requests may be charted as a trend line showing the allocated budget for each month's requests and purchases made. A pivot selection may show these trend lines for each department. Drill-down into any given month will provide the listing of all purchase requisitions, number of bids against each, purchase amount, and deviation from the budget. Another chart may show a pie chart that represents a slice for total purchases from minority-owned small businesses and the rest. A drill-down into the slice may provide details of all purchase orders and amounts within that rollup to the corresponding slice. A stacked chart may show year-to-date purchases broken out among the three segments of new hardware, new software, and software upgrades, and compared against the annual budget for the three segments. A drill-down on the stacked chart may show the monthly purchases broken out within the same three segments that may further drill down to individual purchase orders.

PART THREE

DASHBOARD
SOFTWARE ASSESSMENT

10

SOFTWARE FEATURES

Dashboard software evaluation demands rigorous due diligence to make an informed decision rather than an impulsive purchase decision with too many oops thereafter.

One of the most influential factors in the success of a dashboard deployment is the dashboard software. Even if a team follows best practices and uses a proven methodology in the process, a dashboard deployment heavily depends on the features within its supporting software. So, it is critical to perform proper due diligence in the evaluation of software before a vendor's software is selected and purchased.

Don't judge a book by its cover. The old adage rings true in this instance. It is not prudent to make software acquisition decisions based on standard, cookie-cutter vendor demos. Instead, the team must insist on a proof-of-concept that reflects a typical use-case scenario specific to the proposed deployment. The software features requiring evaluation may be divided into the following ten major categories:

1. End-user experience
2. User management
3. Drill-down
4. Reporting
5. Data connectivity
6. Alerts
7. Visualization
8. Collaboration
9. System requirements
10. Image capturing and printout

Note that software cost is not included as part of the software evaluation from a merit and feature perspective. Once an effective software evaluation is completed on pure merit, price would be a factor. Chapter 11 deals with the return on investment (ROI) and cost factors that need to be considered in evaluating the total cost of software acquisition.

The relative importance of each of these 10 feature categories would vary case by case, so it is best to develop a custom matrix for each case that reflects the relative priorities in the given situation through a simple point system. A relative weight on a scale of one to ten may be assigned to each category, and then a score on a relative scale of one to four may be assigned to each category. The product of weight and scale (weighted score), when summed across all categories, would give the overall score for the software. Exhibit 10.1 shows a hypothetical evaluation matrix.

It is also important to identify up front any criteria that would warrant elimination. In other words, the team must identify the various features or support requirements that are essential to the deployment, and any insufficiency in those areas would simply eliminate that software from further consideration. The often heard but much overlooked adage truly applies here:

Features	Weight 1–10	Score 1–4	Weighted Score
End-user Experience	8	3.6	28.8
User Management	6	3	18
Drill-down	10	3.5	35
Reporting	7	2.8	19.6
Data Connectivity	5	3.8	19
Alerts	7	3.2	22.4
Visualization	8	2	16
Collaboration	9	1	9
System Requirements	6	4	24
Image Capturing and Printout	5	3.9	19.5
OVERALL			211.3

Exhibit 10.1 Hypothetical Evaluation Matrix for Dashboard Software

"The devil is in the details." The following sections describe in detail what may be expected of the software features in each of the previously outlined categories.

END-USER EXPERIENCE

The dashboard software must provide a user-friendly and intuitive interface for all levels of users. As discussed in Chapter 1, dashboarding solutions must be envisioned for deployment across a wide spectrum within the organization. This means that the user base would vary widely in their level of computer savvy and in their software learning temperament. Therefore, a dashboard software program must be extremely intuitive and dummy proof. Some of the key characteristics requiring evaluation within this area would include the following:

- Intuitive graphical user interface (GUI)
- Web-based
- Performance
- Plug-in requirements
- Multilingual support

Intuitive Graphical User Interface (GUI)

Every dashboard software vendor claims to provide an intuitive GUI, but some are better than others. Therefore, the software evaluation process must seek to re-create and assess a true business-user experience. Role-playing may be an effective mode of evaluation to judge the ease of interaction and the effectiveness of presentation for different end users.

Web-Based

As of the writing of this book, the client-server software era is over. This means that dashboard software must support its full features through a Web-based interface. The dashboard must be accessible through the Web (either within an intranet or extranet) by authorized users accessing through any of the leading Web browsers (e.g., Microsoft's Internet Explorer or Netscape). Further due diligence must be undertaken to determine the different versions of the supported browsers and if those versions fulfill the specific requirements for the organization.

Performance

Dashboard performance refers to the user experience in terms of the response time required for loading a dashboard. Evaluating performance is somewhat subjective, but it is nevertheless an important criterion. The glory of a great dashboard may quickly fade for the user if performance is poor. It is often difficult to test a software's response time in a true production environment during the software evaluation process. In order to more effectively evaluate this feature, the vendor must be willing to provide some validated benchmarks on the subject of performance. Talking to existing clients who have deployed the software may also help the team arrive at an objective evaluation regarding performance. The first step, however, in evaluating performance, is to assess the anticipated level of peak traffic for the planned deployment in order to establish a comparative benchmark. The evaluation team will have to rely on reasonable assumptions regarding the necessary supporting hardware and network capacity.

Plug-in Requirements

Most dashboard software requires browser plug-ins to leverage its visual capabilities. Some of the more popular plug-ins are provided by companies like Macromedia, Adobe, SUN Microsystems, and Microsoft. If the dashboard software demands a plug-in that is not popularly available within current browsers, it often creates an initial hiccup for business users who may not be plug-in savvy. Especially if the dashboard is to be deployed for a widely spread customer base or vendors, it is best to avoid a plug-in dependency because it may generate a lot of user queries, complaints, and a need for greater user support. Macromedia Flash is the most popular of all plug-ins and claims to have more than 98% of browser share and growing. Another issue with plug-ins is their version number. It is important to check the software's plug-in version compatibility with different browser versions.

Multilingual Support

This feature is nice to have, especially if the user base will span several countries with different native languages. For example, an English-only interface may not be received well in France, Spain, Japan, or China. Ideally, the dashboard software must facilitate multilingual support effortlessly by simply providing the preferred language selection in the user profile. Depending on the selected language, the dashboard will present the user interface in the user-specific language.

USER MANAGEMENT

The issue of user management was discussed at length in Chapter 3. For a large and effective deployment, dashboard software must provide efficient management of user group and hierarchies, privilege domain, and content domain. The software should also facilitate effective security implementation and personalization. Some of the key characteristics requiring evaluation within the area of user management are as follows:

- Personalization framework
- User privilege framework
- Dashboard grouping
- Metrics grouping

Personalization Framework

The dashboard software must provide an efficient way for the dashboard experience to be personalized. There are two types of personalization to consider: (1) user driven and (2) template driven.

User-driven personalization means that each user should have the capacity to exercise limited control over the layout of the dashboard and help determine the metrics and alerts that will be displayed to him or her.

Template-driven personalization refers to the capacity of the dashboard software to filter the data based on the user's profile, while simultaneously displaying the dashboard generated from a single template. If the dashboard solution will be deployed across hundreds and thousands of users, the features of template-driven personalization must be closely scrutinized. There is a strong word of caution on this issue: Even some of the industry-leading solutions have fallen short on this feature, and this insufficiency makes a large deployment expensive to deploy and maintain.

User Privilege Framework

An effective dashboard software program must have an administrative component that facilitates the management of user roles, privileges, and groups, as described in Chapter 3. The different roles and restrictions permitted within the software must be evaluated against the specific requirements of the organization. The administration of the user privilege framework must be such that a single administrator could manage, with reasonable ease, the user privilege for an audience of a thousand users during the deployment of the dashboarding solution, if need be.

Dashboard Grouping

The dashboard software must allow dashboard groups to be created in such a way that a group of users (using a privilege framework) may be assigned a group of dashboards. This is a crucial feature for large deployments, in that it eliminates the repetitive task of assigning individual dashboards to each user group.

Metrics Grouping

Metrics grouping is a software feature that helps in security management. If a group of users needs to be denied access to a certain set of metrics, those metrics may be grouped, and access to the metric group may be restricted. For example, a group referred to as financial metrics may be created that would be accessible exclusively by users belonging to the finance group. In this way, any other metric added to this group will automatically be restricted from access by other user groups. Metrics grouping restrictions would override dashboard grouping. If a user group has received access to a dashboard that may contain one or more metrics from a restricted metrics group, those metrics would not be shown to that user for that dashboard.

DRILL-DOWN

Drill-down is an essential characteristic of a dashboard software program in that it helps the user perform self-guided analysis. With drill-down capabilities, clicking on a visual indicator on the dashboard will lead to a more detailed level of information that more fully explains the visual indicator. For example, if a speedometer shows the needle in the red zone, implying poor performance, clicking on the speedometer would lead to another chart or report that provides greater detail behind the metric displayed by the speedometer. Some of the key characteristics requiring evaluation within the area of drill-down are as follows:

- Context
- Multilevel drill-down
- Retracing drill-down path

Context

There are typically two types of drill-down links: (1) simple link and (2) context link.

A simple link leads to a destination chart or report that may be retrieved by clicking on the linked visual display in the dashboard. The destination chart or report is presented to the user without any filtering or enhanced intelligence.

A context link presents the destination chart or report with intelligence, based on the context of the drill-down. For example, a user may click on a U.S. map, and depending on the state on which the user clicks, the destination report or chart shows data relevant to that state only. If the software does not provide context drill-down, then the destination chart will present data for all states. An alternate possibility for such a scenario would be to set up separate links for each state on the map, which would be an inefficient mode of dashboard development in the absence of context drill-down. Some software vendors refer to the context link feature as 'cascading prompt.'

Multilevel Drill-Down

An effective dashboard framework must facilitate multiple levels of drill-down. For example, a user may click on a specific visual indicator to arrive at a destination chart or report. Thereafter, the user should be able to further drill down into that chart or report to arrive at the next chart or report. Such a multilevel drill-down may help, to a limited extent, in building a root-cause analysis. When context is combined with a multilevel drill-down, a user may be able to perform powerful self-guided analysis simply through the drill-down experience.

Retracing Drill-Down Path

The dashboard framework must also facilitate a retracing of the drill-down path. A user should be easily able to get to the previous chart from the destination chart. This recursive capacity helps create a better self-guided analysis experience. If users are not able to retrieve the previous chart easily during a drill-down path, they may lose track of their thought sequence. An inability to retrace may lead to user frustration and a dysfunctional self-guided analysis.

REPORTING

Most dashboard software vendors provide a built-in reporting feature or else facilitate integration with a third-party reporting tool. A dashboard is not inherently a reporting solution, but it should serve as a gateway into a reporting system that meets the organizational needs. Some of the key characteristics that require evaluation in the area of reporting are the following:

- Sorting and filtering
- Online analytical processing (OLAP) features
- Snapshot capture

Sorting and Filtering

A user should be able to sort a report by the different data fields contained in the report. The sorting should be intuitive and also allow for ascending and descending sorts. The reporting framework must also allow for data filtering, whereby users may get a subset of the report based on selected criterion and data value on the report.

OLAP Features

The reporting framework should have common online analytical processing (OLAP) features, because users may want different summaries, computations, and popular statistics for a given report. Some of the commonly used report statistics would be sum, maximum, minimum, average, count, and percentage for the numeric data fields (measures) in the report. The reporting framework must also facilitate data grouping, whereby the report statistics may be computed for different data value groups. For example, the daily report may be grouped by week or month, territory reports may be grouped by regions that contain different territories, and so forth. Users may also want to arrive at computations that require simple mathematical operations across different columns or rows within the report.

Snapshot Capture

The reporting framework must allow a user to save the reported data at a given instant for future reference. This capability is referred to as snapshot capture. Because the dashboard provides updated data per the current status of the supporting database, the dashboard reports are subject to change. However, there may be instances in which a user wants to capture a particular snapshot of the report and keep it for future reference.

DATA CONNECTIVITY

The dashboard software's data connectivity features must align with the specific requirements for each deployment situation. If the dashboard software does not meet the minimum requirements set by the organization for data connectivity, this may well be an elimination criterion. Some of the key characteristics requiring evaluation in the crucial area of data connectivity are as follows:

- Multiple data source connectivity
- Real-time connectivity
- Standard database support

Multiple Data Source Connectivity

In some cases an organization may need to pull data from disparate data sources into a single dashboard. This would demand that the dashboard software has the capability of pulling data from the disparate sources available within the information biosphere of the organization. Sometimes, however, the organization may eliminate the need for this requirement by consolidating disparate data sources into a single database that would serve the dashboard.

Real-Time Connectivity

The dashboard software should be able to pull data live from any standard data source. If the data values in the specific data source serving the dashboard change, those changes must be reflected in the dashboard. However, this does not assume that the data source will contain live transactional data. The point is that the dashboard software must be able to serve the most current data available within the data sources that are directly feeding the information to the dashboard.

Standard Database Support

The dashboard software must be evaluated in relation to the list of databases it may support. The standard databases currently include relational databases such as IBM's DB2, Oracle, Microsoft's SQL Server, Open Source MySQL, and multidimensional databases such as Hyperion's Essbase, MicroStrategy's DSS/Server, and Oracle's Express. The dashboard software must support the specific databases and the versions that will serve as data sources for the dashboard deployment. Moreover, the software must have the ability to accept *tables*, *views*, and *stored procedures* as data sources from the databases.

ALERTS

Effective dashboard software must have a flexible alerts management system. As discussed in Chapter 5, alerts facilitate management by exception. Some of the key characteristics requiring evaluation within the area of alerts are the following:

- Rules engine
- Action and recipient
- Alert management

Rules Engine

The rules engine must facilitate the creation of thresholds for various metrics. The software must facilitate the establishment of a single threshold across time or varying threshold levels with time. Also, the software must allow a percentage variation for thresholds to be placed and to change across time. The software must also allow for the creation of complex rules (a logical combination of two or more rules), as described in Chapter 5.

Action and Recipient

The dashboard software must facilitate different action and recipient selections for alerts. Actions may include dashboard warnings linked to specific reports, user e-mails, pagers, and system commands that trigger other software actions. Recipient selection must allow for the selection of individuals based on profiles and roles within the dashboard framework, as well as specific individuals.

Alert Management

The software must allow users to prioritize and assign various categories and status to alerts. The software must also facilitate a search and sort capability to look up alerts that may have been issued in the past (similar to effective e-mail software).

VISUALIZATION

Visualization is an issue at the heart of good dashboard software. Good visualization can be the difference between information overload and information insight. Commonly used graphs (charts) are one example of visualization. However, present-day technology has raised the bar of visualization beyond commonplace charts and data widgets. The three key characteristics requiring evaluation within the area of visualization are:

1. Visual intelligence
2. Geographic mapping
3. Screen resolution

Visual Intelligence

In the context of dashboards, *visual intelligence* may be defined as the capability of software to provide better insight through intelligently highlighting relevant areas and values on the dashboard in response to a user's cursor movement. Intelligent presentation improves the user's ability to extract information from data. The cognitive sciences have provided empirical evidence to suggest that images must first pass the scrutiny of a person's visual intelligence before going on to his or her rational and emotional intelligence. An effective dashboard, therefore, must deploy techniques to help filter the right information to the user through the funnel of visual intelligence to help the user avoid the sensation of information overload.

Geographic Mapping

The dashboard software must support a collection of geographic maps and must have the ability to plot data on these maps. Maps might include various continents, countries, states within major countries, counties, and metro areas within North America as well as regional configurations such as a collection of states within the United States to indicate a territory or region, a collection of countries to indicate a world region, and so forth. The dashboard software must also allow for color-coding of the map areas to indicate relative metric values.

Screen Resolution

Most Web-based software is optimized for a specific screen resolution. If the user's screen resolution is lower than the software's optimal resolution, scrolling is required to see the full application screen. If the user's screen resolution is higher than the software's optimal resolution, some areas of the user screen may be blank.

It is therefore important to ascertain the optimal screen resolution for the dashboard software and to compare this resolution level against the organization-wide standard. If the software's optimal resolution is lower than that of the organization-at-large, it may be okay, but the opposite case is risky. If the software's optimization resolution is higher than the organization standard, then many users may miss important information displays because they may overlook the scrolling required to see the full span of the dashboard. As of the writing of this book, an optimal screen resolution of 1024×768 would suffice for a significant percentage of the user base.

COLLABORATION

Collaboration extends the dashboard's role from a passive information interface to an active enterprise management console. It transforms the dashboard into a hub of information exchange, task delegation, workflow management, and decision making. The two key characteristics requiring evaluation within the area of collaboration are:

1. Discussion forum
2. Dashboard sharing

Discussion Forum

A discussion forum is an application that allows a thread of communication among several users. It also helps track the date, time, and sequence of discussion threads. The dashboard software may provide a discussion forum integrated with one or more of its components. A discussion forum may be integrated with alerts, charts, reports, and individual dashboards. This helps facilitate communication among those users who have access to a specific component within a dashboard. For example, if an alert for sales below target for a specific territory is created, the territory representative and corresponding regional manager may communicate on the subject. For future reference, all communication regarding that alert may be tracked through the discussion forum linked to that alert.

Dashboard Sharing

This feature allows users to share a specific dashboard view among each other. Unlike sharing an image snapshot, they may share a specific dashboard view to facilitate discussion on a given topic. However, the software program must also allow for built-in checks and balances to avoid unauthorized information access through this feature.

SYSTEM REQUIREMENTS

The IT environment within the organization must support the dashboard software's system requirements. If the dashboard software does not work within the systems infrastructure of the organization, this is another criteria warranting elimination. Some of the key areas requiring evaluation are as follows:

- Operating system
- Application server
- Proprietary platform
- Browser support

Operating System

Some of the major operating systems on the server side that are part of the current IT environment are Microsoft Windows, Sun Solaris, IBM AIX,

UNIX, and Linux. The dashboard software must also support the versions of these operating systems that are supported within the organization. In other words, the operating system requirements for the dashboard software must fall within the domain of supportable systems within the organization.

Application Server

As with the operating system, the application server requirements for the dashboard software must fall within the domain of supportable application servers within the organization. Some of the popular application servers are Windows 2000 and 2003, IBM Websphere, BEA Weblogic, Apache Tomcat, Apple WebObjects, JBoss, SAP AG Application Server, Sun Java Application Server, Oracle Application Server, Macromedia MX, and JRun Servers. There must be a match between the version of the application server on both sides—the dashboard software requirements must also match what is supported within the organization.

Proprietary Platform

Some of the dashboard software may require its own proprietary platform on which to run. Such a platform sometimes helps develop certain unique characteristics within the software that may not be possible while developing in one of the open standards such as Java J2EE or Windows Dot Net (.Net). However, committing to proprietary standards runs the risk of diluting corporate IT standards and goes against the prevailing wisdom of homogeneity and system standardization across the organization.

Browser Support

Assuming that the dashboard solution supports Web-based deployment, it is important to check the browsers supported by the software. Certain features in the software may not be supported on a certain set of browsers. If the organization has those browsers in its mix of users or is not aware of all possible browsers in use among the user base, it is better to select a software package that supports 98% to 99% of the common browser population.

IMAGE CAPTURING AND PRINTOUT

In the software selection process, it is important to check for the dashboard image capturing feature and to evaluate the printout result.

Image Capturing

Information from the dashboard can be more easily shared if a user can convert a dashboard's view into an image that may be easily incorporated into other software. For example, it is helpful if the software allows the user to convert a dashboard view into a PDF or JPEG file format that may be incorporated into a presentation. Sometimes a user may not have access to the live dashboard, but would still like to present the dashboard information. Image capturing comes in handy in such circumstances.

Printout

It is recommended that the software selection team see a printout of the dashboard generated from the dashboard software. The test printout may be on a standard black-and-white laser printer. The use of special plug-ins in dashboard software often renders the printouts of poor quality, and worse, in a poor format. Sometimes the printouts are almost unusable and far removed from the WYSIWYG (what you see is what you get) standard. As much as we fancy that we now live in a paperless world, the fact is that paper is still an essential medium of communication, no less today than it was a decade ago.

COMPREHENSIVE EVALUATION

No dashboard software package may claim to contain all of the features discussed so far. It is therefore important that an evaluation matrix is developed for each deployment scenario that indicates the must-have versus nice-to-have features based on the specific dashboard deployment requirements. Exhibit 10.2 shows a comprehensive matrix that incorporates all of the features discussed in this chapter. This extensive template may be used as a starting point to identify the most important features and accordingly weigh the evaluation scores, as illustrated in Exhibit 10.1.

Besides providing a relative evaluation framework for different software solutions, this matrix should also provide a reference for due diligence during the software evaluation process, ensuring that important features that may affect the dashboard deployment are not overlooked.

Note that in Exhibit 10.2, a "Yes" in the elimination column against a particular feature indicates that the software must provide that feature to be considered as a potential solution. The set of elimination criteria needs to be

Features	Elimination Yes / No	Weight 1–10	Score 1–4	Weighted Score
End-user Experience				
GUI				
Web-based	Yes			
Performance				
Plug-in Requirements				
Multilingual Support				
User Management				
Personalization Framework	Yes			
User Privilege Framework				
Dashboard Grouping				
Metrics Grouping				
Drill-down				
Context	Yes			
Multilevel drill-down				
Retracing drill-down path				
Reporting				
Sorting & Filtering				
OLAP Features				
Snapshot Capture				
Data Connectivity				
Multiple Data Source Connectivity				
Real-time Connectivity	Yes			
Standard Database Support				
Alerts				
Rules Engine				
Action & Recipient				
Alert Management				
Visualization				
Visual Intelligence				
Geographic Mapping				
Screen Resolution				
Collaboration				
Discussion Forum				
Dashboard Sharing				
System Requirements				
Operating System	Yes			
Application Server	Yes			
Proprietary Platform				
Browser Support				
Image Capturing & Printout				
Image Capturing				
Printout				
OVERALL				

Note: The score for each feature may be calculated as the sum or average of scores arrived at from its subfeatures.

Exhibit 10.2 A Comprehensive Evaluation Matrix for Dashboard Software Features

evaluated in each deployment scenario. Also, if a specific feature is not required for a specific deployment, assigning a weight of zero would help keep the overall score comparison more relevant with what features are needed. For example, if the user base was not anticipated to require multilingual support, a weight of zero for that feature would not give one software package an edge over another for a feature that is irrelevant.

Sometimes, the business requirements may necessitate special needs like dashboard software's support for Personal Digital Assistants (PDAs) or the software's ability to save and deliver content offline, when there is no live connectivity to the Internet. The evaluation matrix may be extended to include such special requirements.

11

SOFTWARE ACQUISITION
AND ROI

Cost cutting is essential to keep up with global competitiveness, as long as the cut does not overlook maintaining the competitive edge required for growth.

Although this is the last chapter on a topic directly relevant to best practices for dashboard deployment (the following chapters explore various case studies), the content herein actually deals with the first step in the due diligence process for a dashboard deployment. Once there is an organizational mandate to deploy a dashboard for a certain initiative, such as Balanced Scorecard, enterprise performance management, supply chain, customer service, and so on, four immediate issues must be examined:

1. Build versus buy
2. Software evaluation
3. Cost factors
4. Return on investment (ROI) factors

BUILD VERSUS BUY

Unlike the 1980s and early 1990s, the popular wisdom of the current decade suggests that an organization must adhere to its core competency when it comes to software development. In other words, if a specific software tool does not address the strategic core of what an organization does, the organization is better off finding an external solution rather than building it internally. For example, an online trading or online auction company would be better advised to develop such software internally to contain the intellectual property core to its business. Similarly, if an organization offers logistic services, it is better off developing a supply chain software that is core to its business.

However, when it comes to software that offers other productivity improvements not core to the business, prevailing wisdom dictates that it is better to seek out an external vendor that offers a solution that may best meet the need. Such noncore areas may entail enterprise resource planning (ERP), customer relationship management, database management, business intelligence, regulatory compliance, and so forth.

The build versus buy decision for a dashboard initiative should be measured with the same litmus test as any other software initiative. If the dashboard solution is not at the core of an organization's business, then that organization would be better off outsourcing the solution from a dashboard software vendor.

For the most part, purchasing a dashboard software package makes more sense than building one in-house. It is hard to imagine that a dashboard solution would be the core of business for any organization other than the dashboard software vendors or those software vendors providing vertical solutions such as ERP, process control, or accounting. This leads us to the next important step in due diligence: software evaluation.

SOFTWARE EVALUATION

A successful software evaluation requires mapping the organizational needs to the software features. Chapter 10 included a detailed discussion on software features and a proposed evaluation matrix. The most helpful way to approach the software evaluation process is to begin by documenting all of the requirements for a proposed deployment. Once the requirements are established, it is easier to develop an organization-specific evaluation matrix. Carefully documenting requirements at the outset makes the software search process more productive and helps the team quickly eliminate software that does not meet minimum requirements.

Among the dashboard software options, there are primarily two types: (1) solution specific and (2) dashboard platform.

Solution Specific

Solution-specific vendors specialize in dashboards that are part of the overall approach to specific solutions such as supply chain, ERP, quality control, and Balanced Scorecard. For example, if a company is looking for better visibility and management of its distribution process, a supply chain vendor may have a solution that includes an embedded dashboard interface. This solution may offer all or most of the metrics and process management requirements that are part of the organizational mandate.

However, the usual drawback of such solutions is that the dashboard offering is more rigid in terms of its extensibility. For example, the dashboard may address the supply chain area, but it may not be extended to a marketing dashboard solution because the solution is not intended to support marketing intelligence within the organization. In cases in which the dashboard software could be extended, the cost is very high because it requires custom changes to the software.

The advantage of solution-specific dashboard software is that it is easier and faster to deploy for the specific area. When a company has ERP and supply chain software, the dashboard solution may also have built-in integration to some of the popular software packages. This lowers the initial deployment cost and allows for the possibility of ongoing support when the ERP software goes through future upgrades.

Dashboard Platform

Dashboard platform vendors offer a generic dashboard platform that may be customized to provide any type of dashboard solution. Such software offers a framework to pull data from multiple sources, manage user security and privileges, and deploy dashboard solutions based on requirements. For example, senior management may require enterprise visibility from supply chain, customer service, finance, sales, and marketing. An enterprise dashboard platform can be customized to achieve such deployments.

The drawback of a flexible dashboard platform is that greater initial effort is required to deliver a specific solution. The dashboard platform may also require additional integration work to be able to pull information from existing ERP and/or financial systems deployed within the organization.

The advantage of the dashboard platform is additional flexibility and the option of extending the software into different areas of application that may not be part of the immediate mandate. This may also lead to better standardization across the organization. If a solution-specific approach were taken, each solution area may have separate software vendors, leading to greater software heterogeneity, a condition that is often discouraged by enterprise IT management.

To better compete with solution-specific space, dashboard platform vendors are also offering a growing number of out-of-the-box solutions to reduce the initial deployment cost. Furthermore, some of them may be offering integration modules that alleviate the task of integrating with some of the popular ERP, supply chain, financial, or customer relationship management packages. A happy combination of specific solution offerings within a flexible dashboard platform may be the winning criteria for most dashboard deployments.

COST FACTORS

Like any other software initiative, a dashboard deployment tends to take on a life of its own as part of the organizational infrastructure. So, it is important to get a clear perspective on the total cost of ownership for an extended period. The following are the main cost factors that must be considered for a successful dashboard solution:

- Software cost
- Annual support cost
- Additional hardware cost
- Initial deployment cost
- User training cost
- Ongoing support personnel cost

Software Cost

This refers to the licensing cost of the acquired software. All required components must be considered. If the vendor offers a specific integration module or a specific solution module, the cost of such modules must be included per the requirements. Often, the dashboard software may have prerequisite requirements for other supporting software. In that case, the cost of such prerequisites must be included as part of the total software cost.

There are four common modes of software licensing cost:

1. CPU based
2. Named user based
3. Concurrent user based
4. Departmental or enterprise based

CPU-based software pricing depends on the number of central processing units (CPUs) within the server hardware that would run the dashboard software. There are usually no restrictions on the number of users accessing the application within the organization. In some cases, the licensing also incorporates the processing power and capacity of each CPU. For example, the per-CPU cost for Intel-based Pentium CPUs may be different from 128-bit RISC CPUs.

Named user-based software pricing is the per-user cost for each individual person with an identifiable name who is accessing the software. Such pricing can be effective for a small user base, but the cost may add up if the user base grows. This mode of pricing may also involve a base server price on top of which named user cost is added. In other instances, the software vendor may mandate a purchase of a minimum number of named user licenses.

Concurrent user-based software pricing charges for the number of concurrent users accessing the software. For example, if the license is for 10 concurrent users, it may not allow access to the 11th user. It may be difficult to assess the exact number of concurrent user licenses required for a specific deployment. For effective deployment, an estimate is required for expected concurrent users during peak load (highest number of individuals simultaneously accessing the dashboard). This varies based on the type of dashboard deployed and organizational need. The range for the ratio between the numbers of authorized users versus concurrent users during peak load usually varies between two to five. A good rule of thumb may be to start with one concurrent user per three authorized users.

A concurrent user license may also involve a base server price on top of which concurrent user cost is added. In other instances, the software vendor may mandate a purchase of a minimum number of concurrent user licenses.

Departmental- or enterprise-based licensing allows for unlimited use of the software within a specific department or the organization. There are usually no restrictions on the number or power of CPUs in the server hardware supporting the software nor on the number of users accessing the software. Usually, the only restriction is that the software application must be confined to the organization's internal use.

In some cases, the price of the software may include an additional cost for a developer license. These licenses are based on the number of developer seats required for the developers to create dashboards for regular business users.

Annual Support Cost

Annual support cost includes the licensing cost of annual support and upgrades to the software. Typically, this will range between 15% to 25% of the base software cost with a clause for limited annual increments, if any. The first year's support cost is usually charged with the initial software acquisition cost. The support cost may also vary depending on the level of support selected. For example, one may be able to choose between regular office hours versus round-the-clock ($24 \times 7 \times 365$) premium support.

Additional Hardware Cost

If the existing server capacity is not sufficient to support the additional load of a dashboard deployment, additional computer hardware acquisition may be needed. A large deployment may also require additional data storage and hardware support for development and testing environments. All of these costs must be incorporated into the cost assessment.

Initial Deployment Cost

The initial deployment cost may involve two aspects:

1. Infrastructure readiness (back-end data source preparation)
2. Initial development and testing

Infrastructure readiness may involve back-end data source preparation to ensure that these sources may be gainfully leveraged for extracting information for the dashboard. This process may involve the consolidation of various data sources. This consolidation often leads to some type of extraction-transformation-loading (ETL) process. The cost of such efforts must be incorporated into the assessed cost for a dashboard initiative. This effort to ensure infrastructure readiness will bring with it the added benefits of improved data quality: more reliable and current information.

The initial development and testing process involves developing the initial dashboards. In-house personnel must be trained in the usage of software to create dashboards and also to do performance tuning for a good response time. The process may also require consulting services from the dashboard software vendor for initial knowledge transfer and to gain a full understanding of the software features and best practices for the software. Such consulting costs and internal personnel cost must be accounted for as part of the dashboard cost.

User Training Cost

IT personnel responsible for ongoing software support usually require training in the software administration. In certain situations, users may also require software training to fully adopt the dashboard software. More often, the power users must be trained to best exploit all software features. General business users usually do not require formal training if the dashboard software offers a truly intuitive and user-friendly interface. The total training cost for all user types must be appropriately estimated to avoid any surprises later.

Ongoing Support Personnel Cost

Once the initial dashboards are deployed, there will invariably be a need for IT personnel to monitor and support the dashboard as well as its back-end ETL processes, if any. Furthermore, a large dashboard deployment would also require a business analyst(s) and subject matter experts to continually enhance the quality of the dashboard solution based on user feedback and evolving business needs. Such personnel costs must be well estimated to do justice toward long-term success of the solution.

Exhibit 11.1 provides a cost matrix to develop an accurate estimate for the total cost of ownership.

Note that it is common to have additional users requiring access, as the dashboard is successfully deployed. Therefore, additional software licensing fees (if applicable) may be estimated for subsequent years also.

Cost Factors	1st Yr	2nd Yr	3rd Yr	4th Yr	5th Yr
Software Cost					
CPUs					
Named Users					
Concurrent Users					
Department/Enterprise License					
Developer License					
Prerequisite Software					
Prerequisite - 1					
Prerequisite - 2					
Prerequisite - 3					
Annual Support Cost					
Dashboard Software Support					
Prerequisite Software Support					
Additional Hardware Cost					
Production Server(s)					
Test/Development Server(s)					
Additional Storage					
Initial Deployment Cost					
Infrastructure Readiness (ETL, etc..)					
Dashboard Development - Internal Resources					
Dashboard Development - External Resources					
User Training Cost					
IT Administrator(s) Training					
Power User(s) Training					
Business Users Training					
Ongoing Support Personnel Cost					
IT Personnel Support					
Business Analyst Support					
Developer Support					
TOTAL					

Exhibit 11.1 Cost Matrix to Estimate the Total Cost of Ownership for a Dashboard Deployment

ROI FACTORS

Return on investment (ROI) is a popular measure that is key to driving any organizational initiative and associated financial investment. Any business proposition that has a strong ROI (high rate of return on investment) would generally get the support of management. However, the challenge lies in determining an accurate and reliable ROI. Furthermore, in an environment of competing demands on limited investment resources, how does management determine the relative priorities among a volley of strong ROI projects?

A dashboard initiative also requires an ROI to compete with other initiatives. In any ROI calculation, there are two sources of returns: (1) cost savings and (2) additional business opportunity.

The cost savings factors are the most common in any ROI calculation because it is simpler to anticipate efficiencies and the associated cost of those efficiencies. However, the real winning initiatives are those that may add the significant component of increased business opportunity. Dashboard initiatives may significantly contribute to increased business opportunity when such initiatives are supported with proper strategy and vision.

The following are some of the ROI factors typical to a dashboard initiative:

Cost Savings	**Additional Business Opportunity**
• Reduction or elimination of efforts for consolidating disparate reports • Reduction of time wasted in reviewing overwhelming amount of data and reports • Reduction of time in coordinating and monitoring complex processes • Reduction of effort enforcing regulatory compliances • Elimination of redundancies within the organization for processing of similar data	• Better decision making with more current or live information • Better business insight due to improved data visibility through enhanced visualization • Proactive and timely decision making with exception management and alerts • Greater democratization of information, empowering the front line in the organization • Better customer service and enhanced value delivered to customers and/or vendors

The challenge for determining the ROI of dashboarding initiatives remains in the ability to quantify the applicable benefits and associated monetary value. However, once quantified, it is an easy task to divide the savings by cost factors to assess the ROI.

In a dashboard deployment undertaken by the Supply Chain department of a large auto-parts distribution company, for example, significant improvements in measured metrics were realized within three months. The director of the program commented that the key reason for such a quick improvement was that the personnel within the field suddenly became conscious that their performance metrics were being actively monitored throughout the management hierarchy. Slackness would no longer go unnoticed.

There are some very high ROI numbers (over 500%) published in vendor-sponsored research initiatives. However, the real ROI that would stand up in a court of management scrutiny requires a thorough due diligence for each case. This chapter hopefully will come in handy when conducting such a due diligence process.

There may be situations in which none of the ROI factors drive a dashboard initiative. For example, customer demand, competitive pressure, or competitive advantage may be the driving factors. These factors are extremely difficult to quantify most of the time, but nonetheless are strong drivers for many management initiatives.

PART FOUR

CASE STUDIES

12

DaimlerChrysler Sales and Marketing Dashboard

*We want to steer the company towards where
the stakeholders want us to go.*

—Jeff Nash

DaimlerChrysler's product portfolio ranges from small cars to sports cars and luxury sedans and from versatile vans to heavy-duty trucks or comfortable coaches. DaimlerChrysler's passenger car brands include Maybach, Mercedes-Benz, Chrysler, Jeep, Dodge, and Smart. Commercial vehicle brands include Mercedes-Benz, Freightliner, Sterling, Western Star, and Setra. It offers financial and other automotive services through Daimler-Chrysler Services.

DaimlerChrysler's strategy rests on four pillars: (1) global presence, (2) strong brands, (3) broad product range, and (4) technology leadership. DaimlerChrysler has a global workforce and a global shareholder base. More information about DaimlerChrysler can be found at its company Web site (www.daimlerchrysler.com).

BUSINESS DRIVERS FOR DASHBOARDS

DaimlerChrysler's (DCX) business intelligence strategy has evolved from a 360-degree view of the customer to an enterprise data warehouse to an online analytical process (OLAP) reporting solution and finally to an executive dashboard. All of these capabilities support the vision of a single point of truth for all sales and marketing information and a single user-friendly tool for accessing that information. The ultimate goal is to enhance management's decision-making capabilities.

DCX started with an enterprise data warehouse (EDW) collecting information from sales, marketing, finance, incentive, customer, vehicle, and so forth. The warehouse became the foundation the business intelligence infrastructure was built on. Having accomplished this, the next step was to implement an enterprise reporting solution offered by Business Objects. A 200-user pilot project quickly turned into a 900-user pilot project in a matter of months, largely because of the company's thirst for more timely and actionable information. The business intelligence environment now supports more than 1,500 users throughout Sales and Marketing.

It did not take long to build a repository of more than 1,200 reports, which supply the information needs of many business users. However, these reports were too detailed and too numerous to help senior management easily identify problems and trends. Senior management, at the level of vice president and director, have too many demands on their time to sift through hundreds of pages of reports to find the few bits of information they need to take action on.

SOLUTION

The overwhelming amount of reporting encumbered quick access to the precise and relevant information needs. This drove the need for an executive dashboard to highlight the problem areas, provide custom alerts, and create visual indicators of performance across various divisions, thereby providing senior management with a mechanism to monitor key performance indicators (KPIs) on a daily, weekly, and monthly basis. Just like checking e-mails and voice mails at the start of the day, managers can check their dashboard to get a quick summary of performance metrics against goals.

Exhibits 12.1 to 12.5 provide a sequence of screenshots to demonstrate user navigation through the dashboards.

VENDOR SELECTION

After developing the EDW, it was time to start looking for an OLAP vendor. In-house tools did not meet the performance requirements of Sales and Marketing. The IT department was asked to evaluate and recommend an OLAP vendor. Six best-in-breed vendors were selected for initial consideration.

(text continues on page 184)

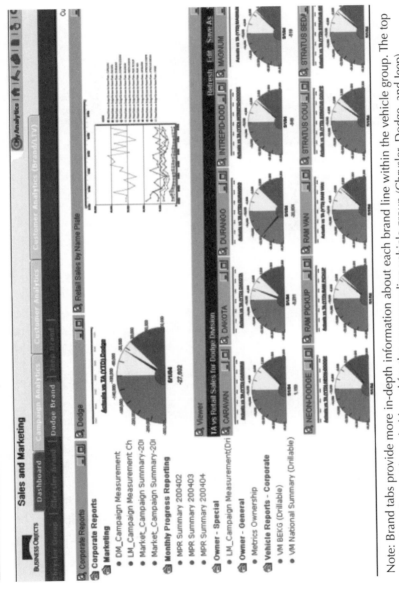

Note: Brand tabs provide more in-depth information about each brand line within the vehicle group. The top navigation tab provides a dashboard for the corresponding vehicle group (Chrysler, Dodge, and Jeep).

EXHIBIT 12.1 HIGH-LEVEL DASHBOARD

179

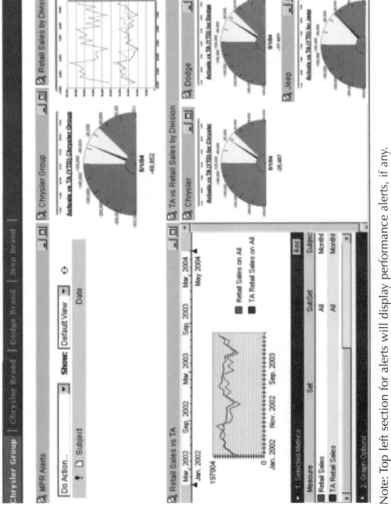

Note: Top left section for alerts will display performance alerts, if any.

EXHIBIT 12.2 SALES AND MARKETING DASHBOARD SHOWING OVERALL SALES AND SALES BROKEN OUT BY VEHICLE GROUP: CHRYSLER, DODGE, AND JEEP

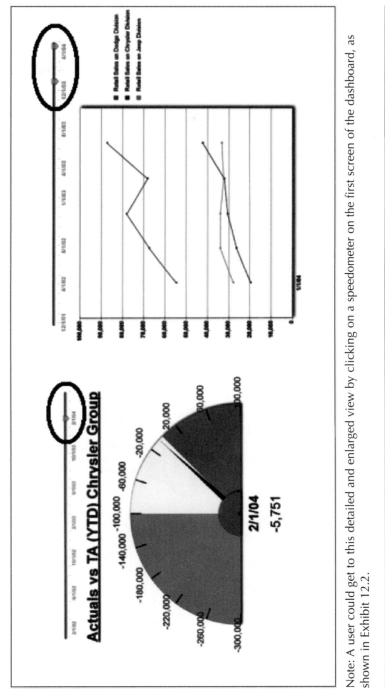

Note: A user could get to this detailed and enlarged view by clicking on a speedometer on the first screen of the dashboard, as shown in Exhibit 12.2.

EXHIBIT 12.3 DYNAMIC SPEEDOMETERS AND CHARTS ALLOW USERS TO CHANGE TIME FRAMES TO EASILY IDENTIFY TRENDS

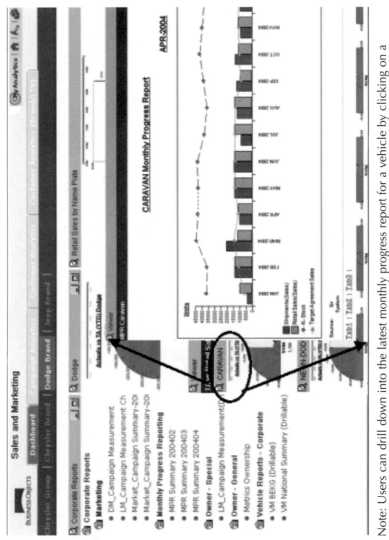

Note: Users can drill down into the latest monthly progress report for a vehicle by clicking on a speedometer for a particular vehicle group, as shown in Exhibit 12.2.

EXHIBIT 12.4 USER INTERFACE ON THE DASHBOARD THAT ALLOWS DRILL-DOWN TO RELEVANT DETAILS AND REPORTS

Viewer

Corporate Reports

Corporate Reports

Marketing
- DM_Campaign Measurement
- LM_Campaign Measurement-Ch
- Market_Campaign Summary-200
- Market_Campaign Summary-200

Monthly Progress Reporting
- MPR Summary 2004Q2
- MPR Summary 2003
- MPR Summary 2004

Owner - Special
- LM_Campaign Measurement(Dri

Owner - General
- Metrics Ownership

Vehicle Group - Corporate
- VM BEKG (Drillable)
- Vehicle Summary (Drillable)

BEKG I By Business Center I DOM %PGM I

Last Refreshed : 19 Jul 2004 07:31 AM

Division	Carline	MTD Sales	Projected Sales	Prior Month Sales	% Change Prior Month	Prior Year Sales	% Change Prior Year	YTD Sales	Days Supply	Total Availability	Avail Days Supply
Chrysler	300C	3,640	10,554	10,341	2.06 %	1,507	(86.13 %)	5,403	13	30,025	74
	300M	195	510	646	(20.99 %)	1,021	(80.55 %)	1,326	68	1,326	68
	CONCORDE	117	321	400	(19.73 %)	255	(464.03 %)	1,473	119	1,473	119
	CROSSFIRE	527	1,446	1,605	(9.89 %)	94	(100.00 %)	8,380	151	16,928	304
	NEON-PLY	0	0	1	(100.00 %)	83	(86.77 %)	7	0	7	0
	PROWLER	4	11	0	21.97 %	2,409	(34.47 %)	128	303	128	303
	SEBRING CONV	575	1,578	1,800	(12.34 %)	547	(32.77 %)	9,213	135	12,040	206
	SEBRING COUPE	134	366	395	(6.90 %)	2,545	(13.63 %)	3,504	248	4,350	306
	SEBRING SEDAN	901	2,199	2,443	(10.02 %)	3,738	6.45 %	9,509	102	15,894	188
	PACIFICA	1,460	3,979	4,882	(16.49 %)			21,378	140	31,878	208
	PT Convertible	654	1,795	1,957	(8.29 %)	8,091	(25.87 %)	9,030	116	16,395	236
	PT CRUISER	2,180	5,991	6,471	(7.42 %)	8,202	7.17 %	17,991	78	36,293	157
	TOWNCTRY	3,203	8,790	9,829	(11.47 %)	1,344	14.90 %	27,156	80	45,181	134
	TOWNCTRY SWB	479	1,314	1,571	(16.33 %)	29,616	31.20 %	4,963	99	7,255	144
Chrysler	Total	14,159	38,956	42,450	(8.47 %)			116,579	78	216,760	147
Dodge	INTREPID	195	538	600	(11.68 %)	1,370	(80.74 %)	1,890	91	1,890	91
	Maxxum	992	1,900	784	142.22 %			4,570	63	15,846	217

EXHIBIT 12.5 DASHBOARD PROVIDES QUICK ACCESS TO THE POPULAR REPORTS THAT ARE AVAILABLE FOR EACH VEHICLE GROUP

Three were eliminated in the first round. Business Objects was selected because of its scalability, compatibility with the existing hardware and software, and ease of use.

The business intelligence team at DCX was first exposed to dashboard technology at the 2002 Business Objects User Conference. The team quickly saw the potential offered by this technology. While the Business Objects reporting tool gained a rapid following in the field and middle management ranks, senior management was largely unaware of the tool. An executive dashboard was the answer, and Business Object's Application Foundation was the tool for the job.

IMPLEMENTATION

When it comes to implementing a new technology, the same process is always followed. First, look for the necessary experience and skills in-house. If it does not exist, bring the necessary experience in from the outside. In the case of the Business Objects implementation, IT employed Business Object's Professional Services group to help with the implementation. An important requirement of any Professional Services contract is knowledge transfer to and training for existing IT staff. The burden of support falls on the existing IT staff once the Professional Services consultants leave.

The same process was followed with the Application Foundation implementation. Business Objects' Professional Services helped with software installation, configuration, and initial prototyping. The internal IT team, working closely with Business Objects' Professional Services, acquired the software skills necessary to support and enhance the dashboards in the future.

An important consideration with any new tool is people's natural resistance to change. Everyone in corporate America today is extremely busy. Launching a new tool can meet with mild to strong resistance because nobody has the time to learn something new. The strategy for managing this natural resistance to change was to start at the top and work down. Senior vice presidents and vice presidents were the first to get the new dashboard. Directors and senior managers are more likely to learn a new tool if they see their boss using the tool.

Meetings with group directors and their teams helped establish dashboard requirements for individual product groups, to assess how they monitor their KPIs. Based on an iterative approach, we developed dashboards for each product group, such as Chrysler, Jeep, and Dodge.

EARLY USER REACTION

Excitement over the dashboard technology is very strong. Everyone recognizes the potential this technology offers to put the right information in the right hands at the right time. However, it is still a new tool, and it will take time to fully realize its true potential.

More important than the tool is the culture. To really be effective, senior management must embrace this new technology into their daily decision-making process. Strategic goals must be measured using this technology. Until that happens, or more accurately *when* that happens, the business intelligence vision will not be truly realized.

LESSONS LEARNED

One area of opportunity related to dashboard design and best practices. Although the software vendor provided people who were good at installing, configuring, and using the software, they did not provide any help in dashboard design or best practices for deploying an enterprise dashboard solution. In retrospect, more time should have been spent evaluating Professional Service providers. Software installation and configuration was not an area of weakness, but executive dashboard design and deployment was.

When DCX started developing its dashboard, there was no standard textbook or guide to follow. As a result, the time-tested trial-and-error method was used, but that is the price one pays for being the early adopters of a technology or a new idea.

THOUGHTS FOR THE FUTURE

The business intelligence group plans to add enhanced features and functions to the executive dashboard. In addition, Performance Manager tools offered by Business Objects and other companies offer the ability to link actual results to corporate goals and strategies. This is a logical next step in DCX's business intelligence evolution.

In the world of *Star Trek*, powerful computers monitor and record every aspect of an event—not just the raw data, but what was said and done in response to the data. That capability is missing in today's business intelligence suite of tools. Today's tools do a very good job of aggregating large amounts of raw data, but the analysis, the discussions, what was done is lost, and that is the most important part. The next evolution of business intelligence tools must address this deficiency. Knowing that sales are down this month or last month is not nearly as important as understanding *why* sales are down and what was done to correct the problem.

What is needed is a black-box for the enterprise that would track all communications among the enterprise pilots, as well as among the pilots and the tower. So, when something happens, the company has a full audit trail of events, similar to the resources Captain Kirk has at his disposal to pilot the *Enterprise*.

13

ING DIRECT EXECUTIVE DASHBOARD

The golden rule is to simplify, simplify, simplify! The easier the
application is to use, the more likely it is to be readily adopted.
                                                              —David Lewis

Headquartered in Wilmington, Delaware, ING DIRECT is the operating
name of ING Bank, fsb (Member FDIC), a federally chartered savings bank
offering the Orange Savings Account, the nation's highest yield with no min-
imums and no fees. ING DIRECT is part of ING (NYSE: ING), one of the
top 25 largest financial organizations in the world, with more than $700 bil-
lion in assets. ING has been operating in the United States for more than 100
years, with more than 11,000 employees working for ING companies.

ING DIRECT USA has more than 2 million customers and more than $30
billion in assets. The phenomenal performance of the company is apparent
from the fact that ING DIRECT was launched in the United States in the fall
of 2000 and has already grown to be one of the eight direct banks operated
globally by ING; the other locations are Canada, Australia, France, Spain,
Italy, the United Kingdom, and Germany (where ING DIRECT is known as
DiBa), with a total worldwide customer base of more than 10 million
(including U.S. customers).

BUSINESS DRIVERS FOR DASHBOARDS

Four key business drivers for dashboards were the following:

1. Monitoring of results
2. Single version of the truth

Cube Date: Tuesday, July 06, 2004 06:34:38 PM

Account Channel ▾	Account Status ▾	Balance Tier ▾	Camp Start Date ▾	**Boston Launch 2002-03** ▾	Close Date ▾	Contact Pur
Creative 2 ▾	Envelope ▾	Geog 1 ▾	Geog 2 ▾	List ▾	Location ▾	Media region ▾	Offer ▾	Open Date ▾	Open Trend ▾
Primary Media ▾	Product ▾	ProductRef ▾	Seg 1 ▾	Seg 2 ▾	Seg 3 ▾	Single/Joint ▾	State ▾	SubProductRef ▾	ASP/PAT

Number of Accounts as values	Number of Accounts	Balance	Drop amount	% Resp	Avg Balance	Est Cost/$	Est Cost/account
DM68A	158	$1,493,863	12,500	1.2640%	$9,455	$.0050	$47
DM68B	3,108	$34,181,646	225,000	1.3813%	$10,998	$.0042	$46
DM68C	189	$2,187,860	12,447	1.5184%	$11,576	$.0037	$43
DM68D	151	$2,263,955	12,500	1.2080%	$14,993	$.0033	$50
DM68E	2,869	$39,172,600	225,000	1.2751%	$13,654	$.0035	$48
DM68F	171	$2,012,780	11,725	1.4584%	$11,771	$.0039	$45
DM68G	425	$5,784,011	25,900	1.6409%	$13,609	$.0032	$43
Boston Launch 2002-03	7,071	$87,096,715	525,072	1.3467%	$12,317	$.0038	$47

Note: Top navigation tab provides access to switch among the different dimensions.

EXHIBIT 13.1 DASHBOARD INTERFACE THAT ALLOWS EASY VIEWING AND ANALYSIS OF THE RESULTS OF MARKETING ACTIVITY WITH MORE THAN 30 DIFFERENT DATA DIMENSIONS

3. Measurement of deliverables

4. Cost reduction through automation

Monitoring of results: Business managers wanted to easily monitor results to quickly respond and adjust the course of business as needed. For example, company management wanted to monitor the direct mail results (see Exhibit 13.1). Users can easily view and analyze the results of marketing activity with more than 30 different data dimensions.

Single version of the truth: Different managers arrived at different numbers for the same metrics being reported in various reports. This led to wasted resources in validation and a lack of conviction about the available information. We needed a solution to unify the various information sources with a common gateway for information delivery. Dashboards helped deliver accurate information to multiple people across multiple departments within the company (see Exhibit 13.2).

Measured deliverables have a higher chance of success. Company management wanted a clear set of measurable goals that would be displayed and well conveyed across the organization. Dashboards enhanced management's ability to get all managers within the organization to focus on the top-priority deliverables (see Exhibit 13.3).

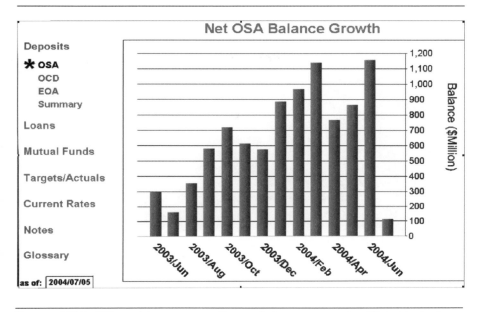

EXHIBIT 13.2 "DAILY MANAGEMENT REPORT" ACCESSED BY ALL DEPARTMENTS

Automation reduces cost. On average, we had two people in each of the ten different departments spending all of their time manually processing and crunching numbers. We wanted to leverage technology to introduce greater efficiency. Dashboard deployment helped achieve greater automation and reduced the number to six people who now maintain the process for all ten departments. The automation has led to far fewer errors as well.

VENDOR SELECTION

There were four key criteria and feature requirements during the vendor selection process:

1. Web based for ease of access, administration, upgrades, security, and so on
2. Industry standard to ensure that experienced resources could be hired
3. Recognized and well-respected leader in the online analytical processing field

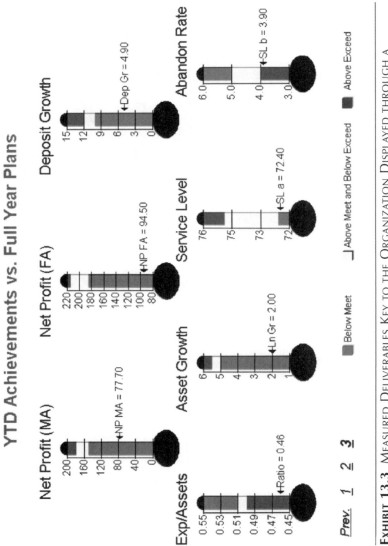

YTD Achievements vs. Full Year Plans

Net Profit (MA)   Net Profit (FA)   Deposit Growth

Exp/Assets   Asset Growth   Service Level   Abandon Rate

Prev. *1* *2* **3**

■ Below Meet   ⌐ Above Meet and Below Exceed   ■ Above Exceed

EXHIBIT 13.3 MEASURED DELIVERABLES KEY TO THE ORGANIZATION DISPLAYED THROUGH A DASHBOARD

4. Company that spends a better than average percentage of revenues on R&D to ensure that applications remain competitive

The two finalists in the selection process were the two most well-known and universally recognized leaders in the OLAP/dashboard space: Business Objects and Cognos. Cognos was chosen because the company had several internal resources with in-depth experience in Cognos's software suite.

IMPLEMENTATION

IT was fully involved from the beginning because dashboards were just one of many important applications that needed to have a steady flow of high-quality information. IT built a corporate-wide data warehouse that is used to satisfy the key business drivers listed previously. Subsequently, multiple other applications were implemented using the same data source. It was very important to build the dashboards first because the OLAP/dashboards became crucial components of the user acceptance testing for these new applications.

Implementation never really ends because managers continually want as much information as they can obtain. New products and services are added, mergers and acquisitions take place, and dashboards at ING DIRECT are used to support every department in the company. If the data are available, it takes the IT team on average four to six months to automate the reporting and analysis for one department (see Exhibit 13.4).

EARLY USER REACTION

Early user reaction was and continues to be enthusiastic. Dashboards and OLAP enabled managers to do their jobs more efficiently. It saves many of them from having to manually generate the information and allows them to think about the results instead.

User desire for data in higher volumes, frequencies, and quality seems to have no bounds. Dashboards allow for the presentation of real-time results such that managers can really feel the pulse of the business and easily access a wealth of information, but still they want more.

We have kept development focus on solving specific business issues and answering specific business questions. The early adopters eagerly show the other managers and use spreads quickly.

EXHIBIT 13.4 DEPARTMENT'S REPORTING AND DASHBOARD NEEDS ACROSS VARIOUS AREAS

LESSONS LEARNED

The major lesson learned is that there are many different types of managers whose capacity to digest information in different ways is endless. Some power users jump right in, but most users do not have the time or motivation to learn new software applications. The golden rule is to simplify, simplify, simplify! The easier the application is to use, the more likely it is to be readily adopted. We ended up creating dashboards and OLAP for multiple user levels.

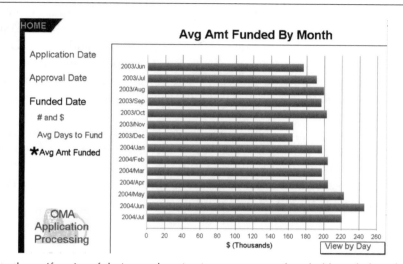

Note the uniformity of design and navigation as compared to dashboards for other areas (such as the daily management dashboard shown in Exhibit 13.2).

EXHIBIT 13.5 EXAMPLE OF A CREDIT DASHBOARD SHOWING AVERAGE AMOUNT FUNDED BY MONTH

Uniformity is crucial. Table of contents, user guides, icons, menus, graphics, FAQs, and the look and feel of dashboards should all be very similar. The finance manager should be able to easily drive the credit or treasury dashboard because it looks and behaves similarly to the finance dashboard.

It is a common theme to have a HOME button to take the user to a table of contents. A table of contents also appears to the left of the information, and the section and page the user is viewing is highlighted in a different color (see Exhibit 13.5).

THOUGHTS FOR THE FUTURE

Dashboards will evolve to become even more intelligent and an even more important tool for managers. They will be able to provide automated alerts that send an e-mail or text message to users, triggers that automatically run a report or complete an analysis, automated modeling that will generate additional results based on what the manager is analyzing, suggestions of what business users might want to view based on recent changes in the data, links to powerful models or other information sources, and so on. Dashboards will be the predominant way for people to receive communication on the results of their computer programs. The closer computer programs and applications simulate true artificial intelligence, the more important dashboards will become.

Exhibits 13.6 and 13.7 show a dashboard example with real-time result monitoring of an Internet campaign. It provides actual results versus a control group and automatically calculated lift, plus real-time modeling results letting the manager know what customer profile characteristics are considered to be the most important for this offer.

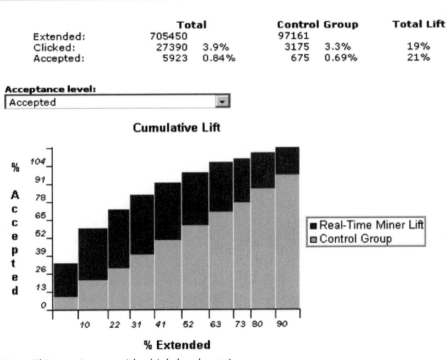

Note: This preview provides high-level metrics.

EXHIBIT 13.6 REAL-TIME MONITORING FOR THE RESULTS OF AN INTERNET MARKETING CAMPAIGN

```
Extended:      705446           -
Clicked:        27390   3.9%
Accepted:        5923   0.84%
```

Acceptance level or transition:

Accepted	▼

The table below shows how different fields affect the likelihood of acceptance of offer *ESTMT_*

Select a profile field to display relative impacts of its values:

Profile Field	Influence ▽		Max Impact	
Visits	30%		70	
OIABalAvgYTD	28%		0	
OIABalAvgLTD	28%		0	
RFMTotalScore	26%		26	
RFMMonetary	26%		24	
DepositAllLTD	25%		47	
DepositAllYTD	23%		31	
DaysSinceLastVisit	22%		69	
WithdrawAllYTD	22%		25	
PreferedChannel	21%		16	
WithdrawAllLTD	20%		27	
RFMFrequency	19%		11	
RFMRecency	19%		14	
ProfitGroup	17%		17	
OCDBalAvgLTD	15%		0	
OCDBalAvgYTD	15%		0	
CIFCreateDays	15%		53	
ClientSinceDays	15%		56	
VehicleNewCarBuyer	14%		0	
OCDMaturityDays	14%		0	
WithdrawAllMTD	13%		8	
VehicleAggregateValue	13%		0	
HomeOwnerFlag	13%		2	
HomeMarketValue	13%		0	
HomeLTVRange	12%		0	
ReferralBonusLTD	12%		7	
HHEstIncomeCD	12%		0	
DepositAllMTD	12%		8	
HomeLOR	12%		0	
HomeYearBuilt	12%		76	
HHNetWorthInd	12%		0	

EXHIBIT 13.7 DETAILED DRILL-DOWN WITH REAL-TIME MONITORING OF THE RESULTS OF AN INTERNET MARKETING CAMPAIGN

14

DASHBOARD IN HEALTH CARE
(EMERGENCY MEDICAL ASSOCIATES)

Once you understand the business at hand, just go and construct a few dashboards for others to critique. It is easier to throw darts at a target than a blank wall.

—Jonathan Rothman

Emergency Medical Associates (EMA) is a democratically structured, 100% physician-owned and -managed emergency medicine physician group that has been providing services to hospitals and health systems since 1977. Hospitals that wish to not directly employ their own Emergency Department (ED) physicians contract with a company similar to EMA.

EMA currently has more than 170 physician owners and employs around another 40 per diem physicians and 60 physician extenders (physician assistants/nurse practitioners). EMA currently staffs 17 EDs throughout New Jersey and New York State and treats more than 650,000 patients annually, all of whom are tracked through their patient tracking and documentation system, Emergency Department Information Manager (EDIM). Each patient record is then fed into EMA's data warehouse, the Emergency Medicine Analysis and Reporting System (eMARS), which is now home to more than 5 million patient encounters. The data provided by eMARS enables hospital administrators to more accurately determine what affects a patient's level of satisfaction with ED services provided, by linking that data across different dashboards. eMARS is also used to provide syndromic surveillance data to the state of New York and New Jersey Departments of Health and the Centers for Disease Control (CDC).

Finally, EMA owns its own management services organization and physician billing company, Alpha Physician Resources (APR) and Bravo Reimbursement Specialists (BRS). Combined, both organizations employ around 180 support staff members.

BUSINESS DRIVERS FOR DASHBOARDS

As a historical perspective on how data management activities evolved at EMA over the years, EMA's investment initially focused on the development and deployment of operational systems used to run clinical and financial business:

- A patient tracking electronic medical record system named Emergency Department Information Manager (EDIM) that resides in each ED in which EMA has a contract
- A homegrown physician claims billing package

In 1994, EMA expanded its data management investment by electronically gathering demographic data from its geographically dispersed EDIM systems on a nightly basis for the purpose of loading this data into a centralized billing system.

In 1998, EMA began a pilot project with the goal of combining data for one site's EDIM and billing databases. This served as the basis from which its data warehouse, clinical, and business intelligence (BI) product, Emergency Medicine Analysis and Reporting System (eMARS), has been developed and implemented. eMARS has been developed to put information in the hands of ED managers to improve operational efficiency, patient satisfaction, and clinical and financial performance.

The business drivers for data warehouse development included the following:

- Dramatic increase in ED volume in the 1990s, leading to a decrease in:
  - ED operational performance
  - Patient satisfaction results
- Dramatic increase in managed care penetration in New Jersey in the 1990s, leading to a decrease in:
  - Reimbursement for ED services
  - Physician incomes
- Dramatic increase in malpractice premiums in New Jersey in the 1990s, leading to a decrease in physician incomes

Six years later, this data warehouse stored information for more than 5 million EMA ED visits in an Oracle data warehouse and offers its physician directors/associate directors and contracted hospital administration personnel two distinct monthly reporting packages via electronic format. Built using Business Objects technology, eMARS services (ad hoc reporting) and monthly analytics became a staple in all EDs managed by EMA and supported many research projects completed by EMA's not-for-profit research foundation.

Over the years, EMA's data management infrastructure became so comprehensive that eMARS monthly packages grew to more than 35 pages. Exhibit 14.1 displays the legend for a typical monthly reporting package submitted to each of EMA's contracted EDs. Exhibit 14.2 displays one of the standard reports in the monthly package. Many of the standard reports were designed to include as many metrics on one page as possible.

There was an effort to collate large amounts of data and present information in a dashboard-like format within eMARS (see Exhibit 14.3). The problem with such displays was that a 0% change was neither the target nor threshold for each metric value.

VENDOR SELECTION

In July 2003, the organizational goals of EMA's management services shifted. The EMA board put forth a mandate that included the following statements:

- EMA management must develop infrastructure that would allow for movement to self-service capabilities in various areas of the organization.
- EMA management must develop infrastructure that would allow for enhanced ability to link, analyze, present, and make available financial, payroll, and other administrative data.
- EMA management must develop strategies that would allow for future movement of variable costs to fixed costs.

Therefore, EMA sought out BI technologies that:

- Are Web based
- Visually display information in a dashboard format
- Allow for the automation of metric updates
- Would increase EMA administrative personnel (APR) productivity
- Offer spontaneous alerts, e-mails, or pop-ups and next steps based on a predefined workflow when a goal or initiative falls outside of a desired threshold

(text continues on page 203)

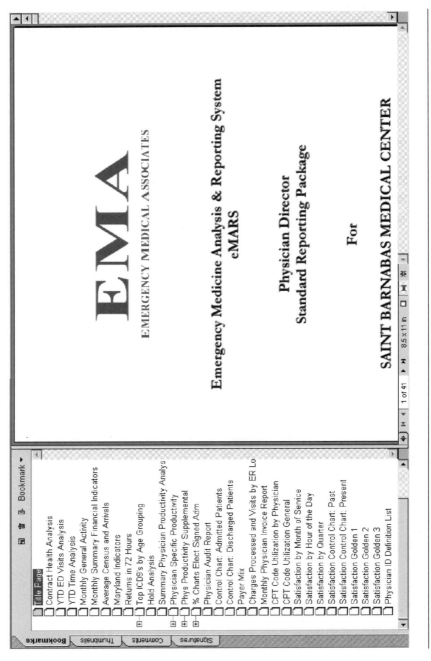

EXHIBIT 14.1 eMARS INTERFACE WITH ACCESS TO MONTHLY REPORTS

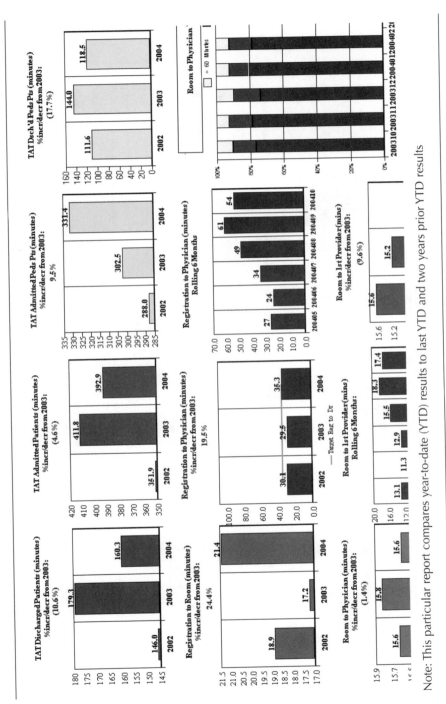

Note: This particular report compares year-to-date (YTD) results to last YTD and two years prior YTD results

EXHIBIT 14.2 A STANDARD EMARS MONTHLY REPORT

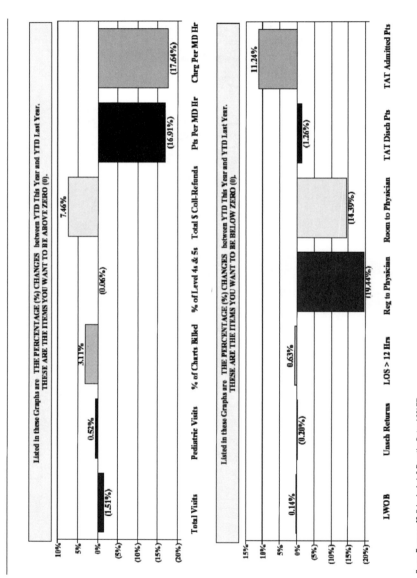

Listed in these Graphs are **THE PERCENTAGE (%) CHANGES** between YTD This Year and YTD Last Year. **THESE ARE THE ITEMS YOU WANT TO BE ABOVE ZERO (0).**

- 10%
- 5%
- 0%
- (5%)
- (10%)
- (15%)
- (20%)

(1.51%) — Total Visits

0.52% — Pediatric Visits

3.11% — % of Charts Billed

(0.06%) — % of Level 4s & 5s

7.46% — Total $ Coll–Refunds

(16.91%) — Pts Per MD Hr

(17.64%) — Chrg Per MD Hr

Listed in these Graphs are **THE PERCENTAGE (%) CHANGES** between YTD This Year and YTD Last Year. **THESE ARE THE ITEMS YOU WANT TO BE BELOW ZERO (0).**

- 15%
- 10%
- 5%
- 0%
- (5%)
- (10%)
- (15%)
- (20%)

0.14% — LWOB

(0.20%) — Unsch Returns

0.63% — LOS > 12 Hrs

(19.44%) — Reg to Physician

(14.39%) — Room to Physician

(1.26%) — TAT Disch Pts

11.24% — TAT Admitted Pts

Source: Emergency Medicine Analysis & Reporting System (eMARS)

EXHIBIT 14.3 A DASHBOARD-LIKE PRESENTATION WITHIN eMARS

Additional criteria set by APR's Information Services department included the following:

- Leverage the existing Business Object infrastructure
- Provide end users the ability to slice and dice information on-the-fly

As a result of these criteria, EMA selected Business Objects' Application Foundation Dashboard Manager as its tool set.

IMPLEMENTATION

Internal Information System challenges for achievement of revised Board goals included the following:

- A small BI staff
- Paralysis by analysis
  - Report packages analyzed everything; targets and alerts were required.
  - Monthly loading of data was not timely enough anymore.
- Demand for new data to be included in BI
- Demand for increased access to data
- Goal of low marginal cost to service new business

An outside consulting group was solicited and employed to:

- Accelerate the implementation process
- Build the foundation for security
- Transfer knowledge

Within three months:

- All technological infrastructure was developed.
- Sample dashboards were developed using existing predefined metrics.
- End users were educated about the new tools and their values.

For an example of how end users were educated about the value of dashboards and dashboard displays, see Exhibit 14.4. Users were guided through samples during the development of targets and thresholds for each dashboard metric (see Exhibit 14.5). Based on users' answers to the questions, infra-

**"Without the establishment of daily alerts,
the real value of loading data into eMARS and moving
to this new tool set will not be exploited.**

**Visually, much of the data will be
displayed on the web site in a "speedometer" format,
with data segmented by color "area."**

In this example, data below 9% is exemplary
and data above 10.25% is bad and above the threshold."

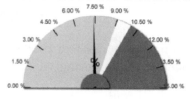

EXHIBIT 14.4 TRAINING END USERS ABOUT DASHBOARD DISPLAYS

structure was developed to send e-mails when thresholds were either not met or exceeded (see Exhibit 14.6). Finally, the entire exercise culminated in the creation of operational dashboards for users to easily manage and monitor their metrics with automated alerts (see Figure 14.7).

EARLY USER REACTION

The first set of dashboards released included the following:

- EMA administration
  - Data views with trending
  - Simple report production with date prompts
- Site (ED) specific
  - Daily ED operations
  - Billing and collection performance
  - Physician salaries (which are tied to collections)

At the outset of dashboard implementation, it became clear that a fair amount of handholding would be required to show our first set of end users,

(text continues on page 208)

Data results are for DOS 1/1/03–1/31/04

Hospital Name	Visits	Visits AMA	AMA %	Visits-LWOB	LWOB %	Visits-Peds < 21	Admit Count	Admit %	Admits-Peds < 21	Admits % Peds < 21	Reg to Room	Room to Phy	Room to First Provider	TAT Adm Pts	TAT Dsch Pts	TAT All Pts
GENERAL HOSPITAL																
Mean	139	2	1.1%	0	0.3%	44	27	19.3%	2	4.7%	21	15	15	409	182	227
Median	137	1	0.8%	0	0.0%	42	27	19.1%	2	4.3%	16	15	14	394	180	219
Minimum	57	0	0.0%	0	0.0%	18	9	8.3%	0	0.0%	7	7	6	239	109	135
Maximum	237	7	5.4%	5	3.0%	110	44	32.8%	7	15.2%	122	26	26	778	268	359

THRESHOLD VALUE																
E-mail me the alert (Y/N)																

EXEMPLARY VALUE																
E-mail me the alert (Y/N)																

EXHIBIT 14.5 A USER SAMPLE TO GUIDE THEM THROUGH THE DEVELOPMENT OF METRIC TARGETS AND THRESHOLDS

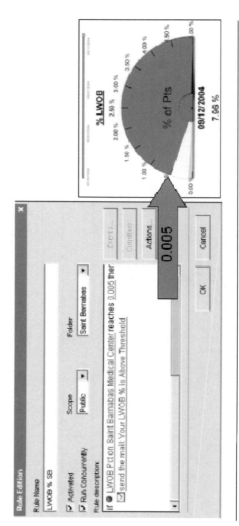

EXHIBIT 14.6 VISUAL PORTRAYAL OF SETTING E-MAIL ALERT ON REACHING A PRESPECIFIED THRESHOLD

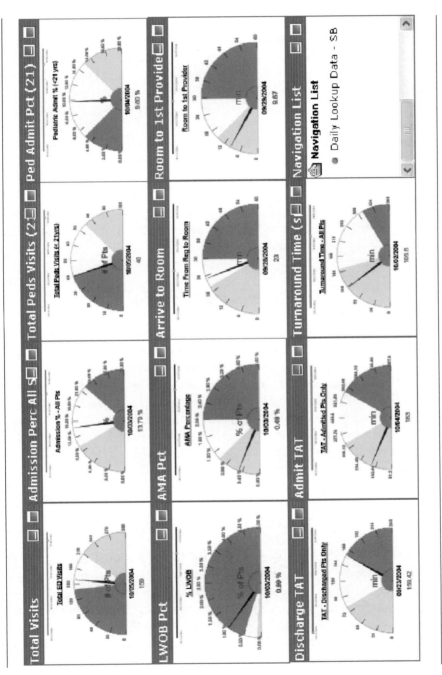

EXHIBIT 14.7 DAILY EMERGENCY DEPARTMENT OPERATIONAL DASHBOARD

physician ED directors, how to use the new tools. A big frustration for end users arose when they were told to go to the Web site to get answers to their simple questions rather than calling up a report writer.

At rollout, one-on-one meetings took place to educate end users on the use of the new tools. However, over time some physician directors forgot how to use the new tools and began to insist that report writers send them reports in the same old-fashioned way. However, some physician directors have been proactive in learning how to use and master the new tool sets. For these few, dashboards have been extremely beneficial.

Furthermore, although much effort was invested in creating alerts for the daily ED operations dashboards, not enough effort was placed on developing alerts for billing, collections, and salary metrics.

Finally, dashboards were also released to internal APR administration personnel who support EMA functions. Much of the gain of moving information to the Web for end users to get direct access to all information has been gained with these support employees.

LESSONS LEARNED

If I were to go back in time and reimplement the eMARS dashboards, I would have set up and run a consolidated, one-day educational session for all end users. During this time, I could have provided a training session, received feedback on metric displays and report displays, and could have made changes. It also would have given me an opportunity to learn more, in a large group setting, about what people's expectations were regarding the new tool sets, and whether, regardless of the new goals established by the EMA Board, our physicians were ready to begin getting their information from a Web-based tool.

THOUGHTS FOR THE FUTURE

In the future we will be releasing our daily ED operational dashboards to hospital ED managers. These are non-EMA physicians/employees, and they may have a greater need for daily ED operational dashboards.

In addition, more alerts and follow-up activities will be attached to the financial and physician billing information available. New development will also include innovative metrics that can help our physicians determine how their activities in the ED today will impact their salaries in the future.

INDEX

A

Accounting hierarchies, 31
Accounts receivable/payable, 125, 127
Action selection, facilitation, 156–157
Activity-based costing, 125
Ad hoc analysis, 15
Administrator role, 39
Adobe, 150
Aggregation characteristics. *See* Key
    performance indicators
AIX (IBM), 159
Alert-level control, 43
Alerts, 69, 92, 147, 156–157. *See also*
    Dashboards; Personal alerts;
    Public alerts; Users
  collection, 12
  configuring, 25
  connection. *See* Collaboration
  construction, 116, 122
  creation, 61
  defining, 28–29
  handling, 67
  level, 41
  management, 156, 157
  rules/actions, 12
  system, characteristic, 62–64
  triggering, 62
  types, 66
  user handling, 66–67

Alpha Physician Resources (APR), 197
  productivity, 199
Analyst role, 39
Analytical domains, 52
Animation
  relevance, 46–50
  usage, 28
Apache Tomcat, 160
APIs. *See* Application programming inter-
    faces
Application
  dashboards, 97, 105–107
  server, 159, 160
  vendor, 107
Application programming interfaces (APIs),
    18
Application Server (Oracle), 160
Applications, embedded dashboards (inclu-
    sion). *See* Custom applications
APR. *See* Alpha Physician Resources
Assembly lines, real-time performance, 103
Assembly operations, 137
Assembly-line monitoring dashboards, 103
Asset management, 107
Attention-getting actions, 28
Audience, 69
  defining, 35
Audio signals, sending, 64
Audiovisual alerter, 103

209

Audit control, 125
Automation, impact, 189

B
B2B. *See* Business-to-business
B2C. *See* Business-to-consumer
Back-end data source preparation, 170
Background colors, usage, 46
Balanced Scorecard, 3, 6, 99, 165–166
BAM. *See* Business Activity Monitoring
Bar charts, usage, 114
Bars, color, 47
BEA Weblogic, 160
Benchmarks, 92. *See also* User-friendly
        application
    collection, 12
    establishment. *See* Performance
    expectation, 109
Best-in-breed vendors, 178
BI. *See* Business Intelligence
Bio-informatics analysis, 107
Blackout management, 105
Blinking, usage, 28
BPM. *See* Business Performance Management
Brand establishment, timing, 93
Branding, 87, 92–93
Bravo Reimbursement Specialists (BRS),
        197–198
Browser support, 159, 160
Bubble charts, 47, 122
Built-in checks, 159
Business accounts, thresholds, 26
Business Activity Monitoring (BAM), 3, 26,
        29
    console, 65
Business analysts, usage, 87
Business areas, 99
Business dashboard, logos (prominence),
        46
Business domain, 61
Business drivers. *See* DaimlerChrysler;
        Emergency Medical Associates; ING
        DIRECT
Business group, 70
Business Intelligence (BI), 13
    evolution, 185
    expert, usage, 87

infrastructure, 17
    maturity, 37
    product, 198
    staff, 203
    system, building, 17
    vendors, 5
Business Objects, 5, 191
    Professional Services, 184
    User Conference, 184
Business Performance Management (BPM),
        3
Business segments, 97
Business stakeholders, involvement, 75
Business unit, 101. *See also* Strategic business
        units
Business user role, 39
Business-to-business (B2B) companies, 107
Business-to-consumer (B2C) companies,
        107
Business-user experience, 149

C
Calculation, usage, 17, 23–24
Call center operations, 137
Capability Maturity Model (CMM), 91
Capital expenditure, 134
Capture. *See* Snapshot capture
Cash out flow, 125
Category Sales, pie chart, 116
Category tab, creation, 38
Central processing unit (CPU), 105
    CPU-based licensing cost, 168–169
CFO. *See* Chief Financial Officer
Champy, James, 111
Charitable/social operations, 137
Charts
    images, usage, 75
    level, 41
    selection, 46
        obviousness, 47
    types, 46–47, 85
        selection, 45
Chief Financial Officer (CFO), 125
Chief Technology Officer (CTO), 105
Client-server software, 149
CMM. *See* Capability Maturity Model
Cognos, 5, 191

Collaboration, 147, 158–159
  system, alert connection, 67
Collections, management, 42
Collins, Jim, 59, 67
Colors. *See* Screen
  palette, interference, 46
  usage, 89. *See also* Background colors
Combination chart, 132–133
Comflex syndrome, 61
Commodity trading, 107
Communication, posting, 38
Companies/vendors, virtual integration
  (creation), 109
Company-specific structures. *See* Rollups
Company-wide purchases, 107
Compliance control, 9
Computer resolution, 52
  considerations, 50
Computing resource utilization monitoring,
  103
  dashboards, 105
Concurrent user-based licensing cost,
  168–169
Connectivity. *See* Data connectivity; Multiple
  data source connectivity; Real-time
  connectivity
Consulting operations, 137
Consumer accounts, thresholds, 26–27
Content
  differentiation, 46
  domain, 35, 40–43
  features. *See* E-mails
  placement, 46, 50
Context
  drill-down, 54, 56–57
  link, 153
  linking capability, 56
  selection, 50, 52–53
Contractors, 132
Copyright symbols, usage, 89
Corporate compliance, 5
  laws, 97
Corporate Performance Management, 3
Cost components, 134
Cost control, 125
Cost factors, 165
Cost matrix, 171

CPU. *See* Central processing unit
Critical alert, 66
CRM. *See* Customer Relationship
  Management
Cross-buying analysis, 121
Cross-buying behavior, analysis, 122
CS. *See* Customer service
CTO. *See* Chief Technology Officer
Custom applications, embedded dashboards
  (inclusion), 107
Customer dashboards, 97, 107–109
Customer Relationship Management (CRM), 7
  dashboards, 85
Customer satisfaction/costs, 128
Customer service (CS), 165
  account manager, 131
  areas, 21
  dashboards, 113, 131–132
  group, 78
  KPIs, 16
  Percentage Resolution, impact, 26–27
  scenario, 131–132
  support/troubleshooting, 131
Customer survey/feedback, 131
Customer-specific dashboard, 131

D

Daily sales monitoring, 62
DaimlerChrysler (DCX)
  dashboards
    business drivers, 177–178
    lessons, 185
    solutions, 178
    user reaction, 185
  future, 185–186
  sales/marketing dashboard, 177
  technology implementation, 184
  vendor selection, 178–184
Damaged goods, rate, 127
Dashboard software, 18, 47
  experts, 75
    usage, 87
  facilitation. *See* E-mails
  features, 40, 147
  packages, 50, 54
Dashboarding initiatives, ROI determination,
  173

Dashboarding process, 15, 69
  groups, role, 36–37
  hierarchies
    impact, 31–32
    role, 36–37
Dashboarding project, 90
Dashboarding software, 92
  selection, 91
Dashboarding team, composition, 91
Dashboards, 5. *See also* Enterprise dashboards
  aesthetic appeal, 45
  aircraft inspiration, 5–7
  alerts, 59
  architecture, 33
  building blocks, 42
  business drivers. *See* DaimlerChrysler;
      Emergency Medical Associates; ING
      DIRECT
  categories, 97
    framework, 109
  contrast. *See* Portals
  creation, 38
  cross-sections, 73
  deployment, 38, 156. *See also* Geographic
      grains
    success, ensuring, 52
  design, 45–50, 114, 122, 127–128
  development, 153
  enterprise-wide deployment, 11
  evaluation matrix, 161–163
  extrapolation, 116
  facilitation, 59
  functions, 37
  grouping, 151, 152
    category, creation, 39
    creation, 54
    identification, 69
  groups
    determination, 78
    privilege matrix, determination, 78
    usage. *See* Privileges; Restrictions
  hierarchy, 78
    creation, 54
  layout, 31, 50–53
    sketch, 69, 78
  level, 41
  link, 63

  misperceptions, 10–12. *See also* Enterprise
      dashboards
  modification, 38
  navigation, 31, 54–57
    aspects, 32
  performance, 150
  personalization, 35, 40
  pixel limitations, 52
  platform, 166–168
    flexibility, drawback, 167
  presentation, 9
  purpose, 12
  refresh frequency, determination, 38
  scenarios. *See* Quality control
  screen, 54
    overloading, 50
  sharing, 158, 159
  simplicity. *See* Information
  solution, design, 24
  support, 11
  term, usage, 5–6
  usage. *See* Health care; Reports; Senior
      executives
  user, 65
    creation, 38
    deployment, 91
  value/effectiveness, 12
  viewer, overwhelming (problems),
      50–51
  visualization, power, 45
  windows/frames, number, 50
Data analysis
  capabilities, 3–5
  delegation, 4
Data connectivity, 147, 155–156
Data elements, requirement, 22
Data formats, readiness, 91
Data grouping, facilitation, 154
Data mining capabilities, 3–5
Data point parameter. *See* Source data point
    parameter
Data redundancies, 17–18
Data restrictions, 9
Data sources, 17–20
  connection, defining, 38
  connectivity. *See* Multiple data source
      connectivity

involvement. *See* Key performance
    indicators
KPI extraction, 23
relational databases, inclusion, 18
Data updates, 64
Data validation, absence, 17
Data value groups, computation, 154
Data warehouse. *See* Enterprise data warehouse
    enhancement, 18
Database
    connection, defining, 38
    profession, 15
    resources, privilege, 37
    support, 155, 156
Database administrator
    experience, 37
    usage, 87
DB2, 156
Debt analysis, 125
Definitions, 12
Departmental cost, 125
Departmental-based licensing cost, 168–169
Department/Business Unit SME, usage, 87
Deployment
    cost, 168. *See also* Software
        reduction, 167–168
    phase, 89
Depreciation metrics, 134
Design, 45. *See also* Dashboards
Desktop monitors, size, 52
Destination charts, acceptance, 56
Developer tools, 78
Dials
    graphic, usage, 28
    usage, 47
Direct business, management, 11
Disclaimers, usage, 89
Discussion forum, 158, 159
Disease outbreaks, 105
Disk utilization, 105
Distribution schemes, 105
Distribution time, 127
Diversity goals. *See* Vendors
Divisional dashboards, 97, 101–102, 113
    areas, 101
    categories, 113
    deployment, 113

Donuts, usage, 47
Dot Net (Windows), 160
Drag-and-drop editing, 50
Drill-down, 92, 147, 152–154. *See also* Multi-
    level drill-down
    links, types, 153
    scenario, 74
Drill-down path
    determination, 32, 56–57
    navigation, 22
    retracing, 153–154
Drop-down lists, 56
DSS/Server (MicroStrategy), 156
Due diligence, 91, 149

E
Early warning system (EWS), 61–62
E-commerce, application, 12
EDIM. *See* Emergency Department Informa-
    tion Manager
EDW. *See* Enterprise data warehouse
Electrical grid monitoring, 103
    dashboards, 105
Elimination
    criteria, set, 161, 163
Elmination
    column, usage, 161, 163
EMA. *See* Emergency Medical Associates
E-mails
    action, 64
    content (definition), dashboard software
        facilitation, 63–64
    content features, 63
    generation, 43
    receiving, ability, 67
    report, attachment/embedding, 63
    software, 157
Embedded dashboards, inclusion. *See* Custom
    applications
Emergency Department Information Manager
    (EDIM), 197–198
Emergency Medical Associates (EMA)
    administration, 204
    dashboards, 197
        business drivers, 198–199
        lessons, 208
        user reaction, 204, 208

Emergency Medical Associates *(continued)*
  future, 208
  technology implementation, 203–204
  vendor selection, 199, 203
Emergency Medicine Analysis and Reporting
    System (eMARS), 197–198
  dashboards, reimplementation, 208
  services, 199
Employee costs, 132
Employee satisfaction surveys/feedbacks, 132
End users, 92
  experience, 147, 149–151
  involvement, 91
  learning curve/training, 10
  presentation, effectiveness/interaction, 149
Enterprise dashboards
  business case, 3
  elements, 7–9
  enhancement, 8
  misperceptions, 10–12
Enterprise data warehouse (EDW), 20
  information collection, 178
Enterprise performance
  dashboards, 97–101
Enterprise Performance Management (EPM),
    3, 5, 26, 165
  application, 13
  console, 65
Enterprise Resource Planning (ERP), 7, 166.
    See also Vendor-specific ERP
  system, 29
Enterprise-based licensing cost, 168–169
Enterprise-wide deployment. *See* Dashboards
  execution, time, 89
Enterprise-wide reporting system, existence,
    37–38
EPM. *See* Enterprise Performance
    Management
ERP. *See* Enterprise Resource Planning
Essbase (Hyperion), 156
ETL. *See* Extraction transformation and
    loading
Evaluation matrix, 166. *See also* Dashboards;
    Organization-specific evaluation
    matrix
  usage, 148
EWS. *See* Early warning system

Executive dashboard. *See* ING DIRECT
Expense cycle, 125
Express (Oracle), 156
External vendor, 166
Extraction transformation and loading (ETL)
  procedures, 18
  process, 170–171
Extranet, 149

F
Field sales reporting, logistics, 88
Fill rate, 127
Filtering, 41, 154
Finance dashboards, 101, 113, 125–127
Finance department, 137
Finance hierarchies, 31
Finance KPIs, 7, 16
Financial division scenario, 125, 127
Financial market monitoring, 103
  dashboards, 105
Financial monitoring dashboard, 105
Financial statements, 125
Financial trading, 65
Fonts, usage, 89
Forecasting system, parameters (change), 64
Frames, usage, 50–51
Fraud monitoring dashboards, 103
Functional elements, 46

G
General Electric (GE), SBUs, 101
Geographic grains, dashboard deployment, 24
Geographic mapping, 157, 158
Geographic nodes, 83
Geographic regions, 125
Geographic sales regions, 70
Geography dimension, 21
Geography extension, 21
Geography grain, 20
Google, referral site, 122
Grains
  assessment, 22
  hierarchical relationship, 32
  level. *See* Key performance indicators
  limitation, 22
  rolling. *See* Revenue
  types, 20–21

Granular dimensions, 31
Granularity, 17, 20–23
  dimensions, 29
Graphical user interface (GUI). *See* Intuitive
  GUI
Graphics. *See* Screen
  usage, 89. *See also* Dials; Speedometers
Gross margin, 127
Gross profit, 23
Grouping. *See* Dashboards; Information; Metrics
  category, creation. *See* Dashboards
Grunt work, 90
Guided analysis, 9

H
Hammer, Michael, 109, 111
Hardware
  capacity, support, 150
  costs, 168, 170
Health care
  dashboard usage, 197
  service operations, 137
Hierarchies. *See* Information; Users
  allocation. *See* Privileges
  creation. *See* Dashboards
  defining, 29–33, 38
  development, 35–38
  expansion, 70
  impact. *See* Dashboarding process
  role. *See* Dashboarding process
High-level information needs, 70
High-level KPIs, consolidation, 41
High-level metrics, 99
HOME button, 193
Hosted applications, 78
Human resources dashboards, 101, 113,
  132–134
  scenario, 132–134
Human Resources department, 137
Human resources KPIs, 7, 16
Human validation, ensuring, 29
Hyperion, 5. *See also* Essbase

I
Image capturing, 147, 160–161
IMPACT. *See* Interactive More Personalized
  Analytical Collaborative Trackability

Important alert, 66
Individuals, management, 42
Industry compliance, 10
Industry trend summaries, 121
Industry-leading solutions, 151
Information. *See* Meta-information; Real-time
  information; Right-time information
  biosphere, 17–18. *See also* Organizations
  harmonization, 20
  information disconnects, prevalence,
    88
  dashboard, simplicity, 6–7
  definition, 15–16
  dispersion, 29
  grouping, 54
  hierarchy, 54
  location, 39
  needs, 38. *See also* High-level information
    needs
  presentation, 45
  sources, 7, 17
Information technology (IT), 5, 91
  department, 87
  domain, 51, 52
  environment, 159
  manager, usage, 87
  profession, 15
  resource management, 105
  staff, 184
  standards, dilution, 160
  team, 191
Informational alert, 66
Infrastructure readiness, 170
ING DIRECT
  dashboards
    business drivers, 187–189
    lessons, 192–193
    user reaction, 191
  executive dashboard, 187
  future, 193–195
  technology implementation, 191
  vendor selection, 189–191
Inheritance, 36
Intelligence. *See* Visual intelligence
Interactive More Personalized Analytical
  Collaborative Trackability
  (IMPACT), 8–9

Internal resources, management, 11
Internet campaign, monitoring, 194
Interruption monitoring, 134, 137
Intranet, 149
In-transit inventory, 105, 127
Intuitive GUI, 149
Inventory
    analysis, 105
    levels, system-generated alerts, 29
    turn, 127
ISO9000, 140
Item totals, 24
iViz Group, 5

J
J2EE (Java), 10, 160
JBoss, 160
JDBC, 10
JMS, 10
Job estimates, 142
Journal analysis, 125
JPEG file format, 161

K
Kaplan, Robert S., 6, 13, 99, 111
Key performance indicators (KPIs), 7, 15
    aggregation characteristics, 24
    calculations, examples, 23
    cataloging, 16
    consolidation. *See* High-level KPIs
    data source involvement, 20
    defining, 17–25
    documentation process, 15–16
    elements, 17–25
    extraction, 23. *See also* Data sources
    grain level, 41
        control, 42
    group access, 36
    historical trend, review, 8
    mathematical operation, 23
    monitoring, 178
    presentation, 46
    providing, 113–114
    questions, mapping, 15
    thresholds, defining, 26–28
    types, 16
    usage, 71, 97

    values, knowledge, 26
    viewing, 11
Knowledge transfer, 203

L
Landing page, 121
Laptop screens, size, 52
Layout, 45. *See also* Dashboards
Lead generation, 122
Liautaud, Bernard, 13, 43
    BI comment, 11
Line charts, usage, 132–133
Linux, usage, 10, 160
Loading. *See* Extraction transformation and
        loading
Logos
    prominence. *See* Business dashboard
    usage, 89

M
Macroeconomic indicators, 105
Macromedia Flash, 150
Macromedia MX, 160
Management by exception, promotion, 28
Manager-level users, 73
Manufacturing dashboards, 101, 113, 134–137
    scenario, 134
Manufacturing KPIs, 16
Manufacturing metrics, 134
Manufacturing operations, 137
Manufacturing process monitoring
        dashboards, 103
Manufacturing scorecards, 134
Manufacturing SPC, 140
Map areas, color-coding, 158
Mapping. *See* Geographic mapping
Market share
    information, 36
    point change, 24
Marketing dashboards, 101, 113, 121–125.
        See also DaimlerChrysler
    analytics, inclusion, 121
Marketing division scenario, 121–122
Marketing experience, 93
Marketing KPIs, 7, 16
Marketing metrics, 121
Markets, worldwide presence (division), 70

Matrix development, 148
Media purchase, 121
Menus, organization, 32
Meta-information, 15, 69
Metrics, 13. *See also* High-level metrics
 collection, 12
 display. *See* Speedometers
 grouping, 151, 152
 inclusion, 128
 monitoring, 125, 127
 usage, 70–71. *See also* Sales metric
 viewing. *See* Web metrics
MicroStrategy, 5. *See also* DSS/Server
Milestones, 89
 estimate, 90
Minority-owned small businesses, 144
Monitoring, 62
Month Ago Difference, 25
Monthly Moving Average Revenue, 24
Moore, Gordon, 13
Moore's Law, 3
Mouse-over prompts, 92
Moving average revenue, 23
Multilevel drill-down, 153
Multilingual support, 150–151
Multimedia design, 69
Multiple data source connectivity, 155

N
Name development, 92–93
Named user-based licensing cost, 168–169
National/regional security monitoring, 103
 dashboards, 105
Navigation, 45, 92. *See also* Dashboards;
  Drill-down path
 path, sketch, 74, 83
 sequence, sketch, 69, 83
 tab, creation, 38
Network capacity, 150
Network traffic, 105
Niche vendors, 5
Nodes. *See* Geographic nodes
 intersections, 73
Noetix, 5
Nonaggregate KPIs, 24
Noninteractive marketing campaigns, metrics,
  122

Nonprivileged metrics, blockage, 128, 134
North American regions, storyboarding
  example, 78–85
Norton, David P., 6, 13, 99, 111

O
ODBC, 10
OLAP. *See* Online analytical processing
OLE DB, 10
On-demand computing, 105
Online analytical processing (OLAP),
  191–192
 features, 154
 reporting solution, 177
 sources, 17
Online auction/trading company, 165
Online help documentation, 92
Online trading companies, 107
On-screen warning messages, 43
On-time delivery, 127
Open orders, 131
Open Source MySQL, 156
Open technology, 10
Operating system (OS), 10, 159–160
Operational areas, 99
Operational divisions, 99
Operations dashboards, 101, 113
Operations management dashboards,
  137–140
 scenario, 137, 140
Oracle, 156. *See also* Application Server;
  Express
Order delivery, 131
Order Fulfillment department, 137
Organizational infrastructure, 168
Organizational performance
 enhancement, 12
 measurement methodology, 99
Organization-at-large, 158
Organizations
 information biosphere, 155
 management requirement, 6
Organization-specific evaluation matrix, 166
Organization-wide deployment, problems, 27
OS. *See* Operating system
Out-of-stock inventory, 105
Out-of-the-box solutions, 167

Overheads, 132, 134
Ownership, total cost, 10

P
Pager signals, sending, 64
Parrish, Karen, 11
PDAs. *See* Personal digital assistants
PDF file format, 161
Percent resolution, 23
Percentage change. *See* Revenue
Percentage Resolution, 26
    impact. *See* Customer service
Performance. *See* Dashboards
    benchmark, establishment, 25
    dashboards. *See* Enterprise performance
    evaluation system, 27
    indicators. *See* Key performance indicators
    management. *See* Enterprise dashboards
Per-head productivity/revenue, 132
Permissions, determination, 40
Personal alerts, 65
Personal digital assistants (PDAs), 163
    text messages (creation), 64
Personalization framework. *See* Users
Personnel cost, 170–171. *See also* Support
    personnel cost
Phones, text messages (creation), 64
Pie charts, usage, 114, 122, 132
Pies, color, 47
Pivots, usage, 54–56
P&L. *See* Profit & loss
Platform. *See* Dashboards; Proprietary platform
Plug-in dependency, 150
Plug-in requirements, 150
PMI. *See* Project Management Institute
Portals
    dashboards, contrast, 12–13
    dedication, 12
Posting sequence, tracking ability, 67
Power distribution, 105
Power users, 92
    role, 39
Prerecorded phone calls, sending, 64
Presentation, 45, 69
    software, 75
Printout, 160, 161
Private alert, 66

Privileges. *See* Database resources; Users
    combination, 37
    domain, 35, 38–40
        determination. *See* Users
    enforcement, dashboard groups (usage), 37
    framework. *See* Users
    hierarchy allocation, 36
    matrix, 85
        determination, 69. *See also* Dashboards
    set, collection, 39
Proactive monitoring, 103
Process connections, streamlining, 109
Process controls, specification limits (change),
    64
Process flow, visual indicators, 103
Process/activity monitoring
    dashboards, 97, 103–105
    examples, 103
Product grain, 20
Product requirements, monitoring, 109
Production
    batches, 134
    times, 134
    volume, 134–135
Production planning system, parameters
    (change), 64
Product-level forecast, access, 121
Profiling. *See* Users
    process, 32–33
Profit & loss (P&L), 125
Project identification, 93
Project management, 90–91
Project Management Institute (PMI) method-
    ology, 91
Project manager, usage, 87
Project milestones, 89–90, 92
    prerequisite, 90
Project planning, 87
Proportions. *See* Windows
Proprietary platform, 159, 160
Public alerts, 65–66
Public service operations, 137
Purchase discounts, negotiation, 142
Purchase metrics, 142
Purchase orders
    monitoring, 109
    percentage, 128

Purchase requisition, 125
Purchasing dashboards, 101, 113, 142–144
   scenario, 144
Purchasing funnels, 142

Q
QPR Software, 5
Quality audit, 140
   management, 107
Quality control, 65, 166. *See also* Total quality
   control
   charts, specification limits (change), 64
   dashboards, 101, 113, 140–142
      scenario, 140, 142
Quarter Ago Percentage Change, 25

R
Rapid Application Development (RAD), 91
Real-time connectivity, 155–156
Real-time functionality, 12
Real-time information, 8
Real-time inventory, 105
Real-time performance. *See* Assembly lines
Real-time production status, 134
Recipients, 65–66
   selection
      facilitation, 156–157
      interface, 65
      restrictions, 65–66
Refresh frequency, determination.
   See Dashboards
Regulatory compliance, 125
Relational databases, inclusion.
   See Data sources
Relevance, 41. *See also* Users
Reporting, 147, 154–155
   platform. *See* Vendor-specific reporting
      platform
   system, existence. *See* Enterprise-wide
      reporting system
   tool. *See* Third-party reporting tool
Report-level security, 42
Reports
   distribution, dashboard usage, 11–12
   level, 41
   link, usage, 41–42
Resolution. *See* Screen

Responsibility, domain, 38, 71
Restrictions
   determination, 40
   enforcement, dashboard groups (usage),
      37
Retracing. *See* Drill-down
Return on investment (ROI), 10, 148, 165
   calculation, 172
   determination. *See* Dashboarding initiatives
   factors, 165, 172–173
Returns, outsourced vendor tracking, 88
Revenue
   aggregation, grain rolling, 24
   assessment, 27
   change, 25
   cycle, 125
   ladder, 125
   percentage change, 24
   sum, 23
Right-time information, 8
Risk management, 107
ROI. *See* Return on investment
Roles. *See* Administrator role; Analyst role;
      Business user role; Power user role
   assignment, 39
Rollups, company-specific structures, 29
Rules
   component, 60–63
   engine, 60–63, 156
Rules engine, characteristics, 62

S
Sales dashboards, 101, 113–121. *See also*
      DaimlerChrysler
   metrics, 114
   sales analytics, inclusion, 114
Sales division scenario, 114
Sales KPIs, 7, 16
Sales metric, usage, 13
Sales monitoring. *See* Daily sales monitoring
Sales performance, 97
Sales Reporting tab, 121
Sales trends, 62
SAP AG Application Server, 160
Sarbanes-Oxley Act, 3
SBUs. *See* Strategic business units
Scannell, Ed, 13

Screen
  graphics/colors, 45, 46
  overloading. *See* Dashboards
  resolution, 157, 158
  size. *See* Laptop screens
Section-category segments, 116
Security
  controls, 43
  framework, creation, 40
  policy, permissions, 33
  reference, 40
  restrictions, 33
Self-guided analysis, performing, 152
Senior executives, dashboard usage, 11
Sensors, communication, 18
Server. *See* Application
  applications, 78
Service groupings, 21
Service-level agreements, 131
  monitoring, 107, 109
Services operations, 137
Simple link, 153
Six Sigma, 140
Skill gaps/training, 132, 134
SKU. *See* Stock keeping unit
SMART. *See* Synergetic Monitor Accurate
  Responsive Timely
SMEs. *See* Subject matter experts
Snapshot capture, 155
Software. *See* Presentation
  acquisition, 165
    total cost, evaluation, 148
  administrators, 92
  annual support cost, 169–170
  building/buying, contrast, 165–166
  command, 63
  cost, 168–169
    factors, 165, 168—171
  deployment cost, 170
  development/testing operations, 137
  evaluation, 165–168
  features. *See* Dashboard software
  groups, 83
  heterogeneity, 167
  licensing cost, 168
  process launch/halt, 64
  productivity improvements, 166

response time, 150
roles, 39
rules, application, 9–10
security, administration, 10
Solaris (Sun Microsystems), 159
Solution-specific space, 167–168
Solution-specific vendors, 166–167
Sorting, 154
Source data point parameter, 56
Source requirements, 56
Space allocation, 105
SPC. *See* Statistical process control
Specification limits, change. *See* Process
  controls; Quality control charts
Speedometers
  chart types, 116
  graphic, usage, 28
  metrics, display, 47
  needle, 152
  thresholds, color, 47
  usage, 47
Spreadsheets
  popularity, 5
  usage, 75
SQLServer, 156
Statistical functions, 23
Statistical process control (SPC), 140.
  See also Manufacturing SPC
Stock keeping unit (SKU), 128
Stored procedures, 156
Storyboarding, 69
  example. *See* North American regions
  group exercise, 70
  process, 75
  scenario 1, 70–78
  scenario 2, 78–85
  template, charts (purpose), 74
Strategic business units (SBUs), 99–101.
  See also General Electric
Subject area level, 41
Subject matter expertise, 113
Subject matter experts (SMEs), 87, 171
  absence, 88
  usage. *See* Department/Business Unit SME
Sun Java Application Server, 160
Sun Microsystems, 150. *See also* Solaris
Supplier/partner, 144

Supply chain, 165
  division scenario, 128
  insight, 97
  KPIs, 7, 16
  metrics, 127
  monitoring, 109
  scorecards, 127
Supply chain dashboards, 101, 113, 127–130
  areas/metrics, inclusion, 128
Supply days, 127
Support cost, 168
Support personnel cost, 168, 171
Symmetry. *See* Windows
Synergetic Monitor Accurate Responsive
    Timely (SMART), 8, 99
System administrators, 10
System requirements, 147, 159–160
System-generated alerts. *See* Inventory

T
Tabs
  presentation, 56
  usage, 54–56
Task management, 9
Text messages, creation. *See* Personal digital
    assistants; Phones
Theoris, 5
Thermometer chart types, 127
Third-party reporting tool, 154
Thought sequence, tracking, 154
Thresholds, 8
  color. *See* Speedometers
  defining. *See* Key performance indicators
  definitions, 27
  maintenance, 27
  requirement, 27
Time grain, 20
Time stamp, tracking ability, 67
Total quality control, 140
Traffic generation, 122
Traffic light, 28
  chart types, 127
Traffic metrics. *See* Web page traffic metrics;
    Web traffic metrics
Traffic monitoring, 103
  dashboards, 105
Training. *See* Users

Transformation. *See* Extraction transformation
    and loading
Transshipment, 128
Travel management, 107
Trend lines, usage, 114
Truth, single version, 188
Turnovers, 132
  ratio information, 134

U
Universal Product Code (UPC), 20–21
Unix, usage, 10, 78, 160
Unread alert, 66
UPC. *See* Universal Product Code
USA, dimension, 21
Use-case scenario, 147
User-driven personalization, 151
User-friendliness, 92
User-friendly application, benchmark, 92
User-friendly graphical interface, 60
User-friendly interface, 149
Users
  alerts, 60
  base, 158, 160
  customization, 31
  experience, 22
  feedback, solicitation, 91
  grouping identification, 69
  groups
    administration, 38
    defining, 38
    development, 35–38
    nodes, 73
  handling. *See* Alerts
    interface, 66
  hierarchies, 35
  management, 147, 151–152
  multiple groups, 36
  personalization framework, 151
  privilege, 32–33
    domains, determination, 35
    framework, 151–152
    management, 40
  profiles, 150
    determination, 35
  profiling, 31, 32
  relevance, 32–33

Users *(continued)*
  role. *See* Power users
    management, 151
  training, 92
    cost, 168, 170–171
User-specific language, 151

V
Variance, 17, 24–25
  calculations, 25
Vendors. *See* External vendor; Solution-
    specific vendors
  dashboards, 97, 109–110
  discount factors, 142
  diversity goals, 142
  portal, 109
  quality/timeliness, 142
  reporting interface, 20
  selection. *See* DaimlerChrysler; Emergency
    Medical Associates; ING DIRECT
  term, usage, 144
  volumes, 142
Vendor-specific ERP, 18
Vendor-specific reporting platform, 18
Video signals, sending, 64
Visual intelligence, 157
Visual presentation, maintenance, 51
Visualization, 92, 147, 157–158
Volatility, 27

W
Warehouse/distribution monitoring, 103, 105
  dashboards, 105
Warranty incidents, 131
Weather/climate monitoring, 103
  dashboards, 105

Web browsers, 149
Web business, 127
Web metrics, viewing, 54
Web page traffic metrics, 121
Web Services, 10
Web traffic alerts, 122
Web traffic metrics, 121–122
Web-based interface, 149
Web-based software, optimization, 158
Webinar (Web-based seminar), 92
WebObjects (Apple), 160
Weekly sales
  comparison, 62
  data, 22
What you see is what you get (WYSIWYG),
  161
Windows
  layout, proportion, 51
  limitation, 51
  size, uniformity, 51
  symmetry/proportions, 51
  usage, 50–51
Windows (operating system), usage,
  10, 78
Workflow management, 107
Worldwide dimension, 21
Worldwide sales data, 22

X
XML, 10

Y
Yahoo, referral site, 122
Year ago (YAGO) calculations, 24
Year to date (YTD), 26
Year-to-date purchases, 144

DATE DUE

GAYLORD			PRINTED IN U.S.A.